Scribe Publications
THE TATTOOED FLOWER

Suzy Zail was born in 1966 in Melbourne, and has worked as a solicitor specialising in litigation. After the birth of her first child, Suzy left the law to concentrate on writing. Suzy has written for magazines, and is the author of award-winning children's books. Her children's fiction has been published in Australia, Canada, and the United States.

*To my father, who taught me how to live.
And to my mother, who taught me how to love.
And to my brothers, who lived this story with me.*

THE TATTOOED FLOWER

A MEMOIR

SUZY ZAIL

SCRIBE
Melbourne

Scribe Publications Pty Ltd
PO Box 523
Carlton North, Victoria, Australia 3054
Email: info@scribepub.com.au

First published by Scribe 2006

Copyright © Suzy Zail 2006

All rights reserved. Without limiting the rights under
copyright reserved above, no part of this publication may be
reproduced, stored in or introduced into a retrieval system,
or transmitted, in any form or by any means (electronic,
mechanical, photocopying, recording or otherwise) without
the prior written permission of the publisher of this book.

Edited by Foong Ling Kong
Text designed by Miriam Rosenbloom
Cover image: an aerial reconnaissance photo of Auschwitz concentration
camp, courtesy of the United States Holocaust Memorial Museum
Cover illustration: Cassandra Allen
Cover design: Miriam Rosenbloom
Typeset in Simoncini Garamond 11.25/15.75 pt by the publishers
Printed and bound in Australia by Griffin Press

National Library of Australia
Cataloguing-in-Publication data

Zail, Suzy.
 The tattooed flower.

ISBN 1 920769 76 5

1. Braun, Emil. 2. Holocaust survivors - Australia -
Biography. 3. Jews - Australia - Biography. 4. Immigrants
- Australia - Biography. 5. Fathers and daughters -
Australia - Biography. I. Title.

940.5318092

www.scribepub.com.au

Contents

1	April 1998	1
2	Saturday: Jew-boy	7
3	April 1998	21
4	Sunday: cattle trains	24
5	May 1998	37
6	Monday: A7639	40
7	September 2000	53
8	Tuesday: cavalcade of skeletons	58
9	March 2000	74
10	Wednesday: the taste of chocolate	80
11	February 2002	91
12	Thursday: escape	96
13	April 2002	117
14	Friday: the new Australian	122
15	September 2002	140
16	Saturday: big business	144
17	February 2002	164
18	Sunday: Judy	171
19	April 1998	182
20	December 2001	189
21	November 2002	196
22	February 2003	200
	Acknowledgements	213

One

APRIL 1998

As soon as my father took off his shirt, my brother knew. He knew before all of us. He knew before my father did. Gary had spent the last decade working in respiratory medicine and intensive care. He thought he'd seen it all. Nothing prepared him for this.

My father's arms, exposed and stripped of muscle, hung twitching at his side. He couldn't lift them above his shoulders. Gary looked him over. How had he not noticed the skinny arms, weak neck and shrunken forearms?

'Say, "Ah".'

Gary examined our father's throat, buckling at the sight of the shrivelled, quivering tongue. He pulled out a wooden spatula and gently pressed down on it. No response. He pushed harder—still no gag reflex; then harder. Forcing the back of our father's throat to respond, searching for movement, he didn't realise he was hurting him. He only stopped when our father grabbed his hand.

'What's up?' my father asked.

Gary fumbled in his bag.

Stay vague, he thought. I might be wrong. Please, God, let me be wrong! He ran through a mental checklist — tests needed, see a neurologist, exclude other possibilities, devise a plan of attack.

'I'm not sure. Could be a nerve or muscle problem. I think you should see a neurologist.'

But he was sure. And he cried in his car and later that night in his wife's arms as he remembered the motor neurone patients he'd treated, all now dead. He thought about the feeding tubes and wheelchairs and ventilators, and he thought about not writing the referral. Without a diagnosis the disease had no shape. The truth and pain remained with him.

He sent the referral. It was the hardest letter he ever wrote, because he knew his hunch was right. He knew that as soon the neurologist examined my father, he'd have to tell him he was dying. And then there would be no stopping it.

I try to remember the night my father told us he was dying. He had worked so hard to spare us from pain, to raise positive, confident, loved children untouched by the cruelty and fear that had threatened his life. He wanted us naïve and cushioned from reality. He hated being the cause of our pain, the one to introduce us to illness.

He knew of no other way, but to tell it straight.

'I'm going to die.'

April 1998

He had Motor Neurone Disease.

And six months to live.

❀

I try to remember what it felt like to hear my father tell us he was dying. To recall his pained expression, my mother's wild grief, my brothers' disbelief and my grandmother's panic. But I can't. I only know what it feels like now. To sit next to his silent, stooping frame, hold his waxy, lifeless hand, tell him I love him and search his eyes for a response.

I guess I don't want to remember. I want to stay cushioned.

Small shards of memory remain from the days after my father's revelation. My sister-in-law Lesley stacking the pantry with bottles of herbal medicine, elixirs, pastes and powders. My brother Peter's researched articles on Stephen Hawking, fellow survivor, and my husband Shaun convincing us all of the impossibility of predicting the precise course of a disease. All of us fighting the truth.

My mother and I in the backyard. The garden where I grew up. Sitting in the sun, numb to its warmth, hounding her for a promise. Her promise not to leave us, too.

When I'd asked her how she felt about the diagnosis, I'd expected her to be devastated. I hadn't expected her to say 'I want to go with him.'

I grabbed her. Perhaps a little too hard.

'Please don't say you want to die,' I begged, knowing that a part of her already had.

'Take it back,' I pleaded, scrambling to come up with a

reason why she should. I didn't have one, except that I didn't want to lose her, too.

'We need you. We can't do this alone. Please,' I persisted. 'Promise you'll stay. Say you will. S<small>AY IT</small>.'

She promised. And though she was a woman of her word, I was frightened. Frightened that I couldn't will her to want life, afraid that she may never again find sleep in a half- empty bed, sad that soon she'd feel so alone.

I remember waking one morning at three, switching on the computer and tapping 'Motor Neurone Disease' into an Internet search engine. I remember pressing 'Print' and returning to bed with three sheets of paper. I remember hiding under the covers with a torch, so as not to wake my husband, and seeing the words in print.

Motor Neurone Disease.

No remissions.

No treatment.

No cure.

Average survival time: two to three years.

My father would need help to walk, talk, feed and toilet himself. He would end up paralysed.

The cause of the disease was unknown; the end, a dead certainty.

❦

'I can't believe you don't remember that night,' Shaun responds when I ask him to fill in the blanks.

'I need you to be my memory,' I tell my husband. 'I want to remember how I felt.'

April 1998

'How you felt? It was *all* you felt. The rest—me, the kids, your career, your friends—we dropped away. You just wanted to be with him.'

I remember that. No matter how hard I pretended, Dad was unmistakably, unstoppably dying. I wasn't angry. There was no one to be angry *at*. Dad's illness was just one of those awful, inexplicable things that happen.

I remember crying. Not so much in front of my father. He was so together, so hopeful. It felt wrong to break down in front of him. Part of it was pretence. Mostly I was taking my father's cue, following his lead, getting on with life. It was when I was home, in bed with Shaun, that I cried. In the dark, as he held me silently, not trying to make me feel better, just allowing me to feel.

I felt cheated. For myself and for my father. He was with me now, perhaps more than ever, but with each day I was losing him, so my priority became him. Being with him. Not only in those first comfortless days, but every day. I didn't want to say goodbye, especially to a man I loved but knew so little about.

My father was a busy man. I was busy, too. We loved each other, talked easily and often, but in the end we were like most fathers and daughters—not curious enough about the people we call family, too comfortable in our love for each other to question what we love about each other. Too lazy to ask questions. Too busy to listen.

I had learnt of Dad's approaching death, but what of his life?

I thought about what I did know. I knew he was born in a small town in Czechoslovakia. I couldn't recall its name.

I knew his brother had been killed in the war, but I didn't know how. I knew he was a successful businessman, but not how he'd found success.

So, when my father pulled me aside a few weeks after his world had been blown apart and said, 'Let's not waste the little time left to us. Let's dry our tears and talk instead of cry,' I had to agree.

We fly to Fiji, twelve of us, children and grandchildren. My parents have brought us here to eat, drink, play and laugh together. But mostly we are here to hear my father's story. Our story.

We tuck our children into bed each night of our ten-day island stay and escape to our parents' *bure* next door. My father tells us everything. The words come out in his new, strangely garbled voice, already weakened by the disease. I try to keep the video recorder from shaking as he tells us about his childhood. I zoom in on his face, knowing that soon a three-hour VHS tape is all that I'll have of my father. Gary holds a tape recorder to Dad's lips. Peter scribbles notes. We want to be sure we get this.

My father starts his story on a Saturday.

Two

SATURDAY: JEW-BOY

I was a lonely child. I remember, as early as first grade, watching the other children laugh and play, and wishing they'd talk to me. It was 1936 and I was a Jew. In Czechoslovakia, kids didn't play with Jews. In Porubka they ignored us, or beat us up. They called me 'Jew-boy' and 'Stinking Jew'. I was hated, not for who I was, but because I was born to Jewish parents. It was out of my control, but I wasn't beyond fighting it.

I didn't start out a fighter. At first I tried to fit in. I didn't feel different, but looking in the mirror—skinny boy, skullcap, long ringlets of hair falling from my temples ('*peyot*', we called them)—I could see, to them, I was odd. So I hid my skullcap and cut my hair and looked in the mirror again. No sign of a Jew. I looked at the brown ribbons of hair lying on the floor—six years in the growing, thousands of years of tradition—and knew my father would be angry. I was ready for his fury. I wanted friends.

But 'Tatte'—that's what we called my father—wasn't

angry. Just sad. He sat me down and in a very quiet voice explained hatred.

'Emil,' he said, 'you may look like them, act like them, even talk like them. But to them you are a Jew, and will always be a Jew. You can change your clothes, your hair, even your name, but to the rest of the world you will always be different.'

He chose to be proud of that difference. He hoped that one day I would be, too.

My father was right, as fathers usually are. The taunting continued and the beatings were just as severe with or without my skullcap. I began to understand the depth of my classmates' hatred for me and something inside me hardened. Now, when I was banned from the playground, I didn't hang back. I deserved to play soccer—being Jewish didn't change that. So I marched into the thick of a game and fought for the ball. I still got beaten up every lunchtime, but I made my point.

'Don't go. Don't hide,' I'd plead with my Jewish classmates as, one by one, they retreated to the safety of our classroom. 'If we all stick together,' I begged, 'if we stand up for ourselves, maybe they'll leave us alone.'

But they didn't and I headed out to the soccer game, every recess, alone. I didn't want to fight. I just couldn't give in.

My Jewish classmates said that by refusing to be treated like dirt, I was asking for trouble. Being Jewish was hard enough. Being near me was doubly dangerous, so they stayed away, frightened of my fearlessness. There were fourteen Jewish families in our village. Sixty-seven children. And not one of them talked to me. They didn't call me 'Christ-killer' or pin me to the ground, but their treatment hurt just as much. They reported on each fight to my Hebrew tutor, Mr Wasserman, who delighted in caning me. They ridiculed me by parading around with bandaged heads and gossiped about me to their parents. My only friend was Maria, a plump redhead. Maria never talked to me, but she didn't make fun of me or call me names either.

When my classmates were feeling especially feisty they'd coax Janco to beat me up. Janco was mentally handicapped, but on the playground social ladder, he was one rung up from me. Like a puppy dog, innocent and eager, Janco gave me his best, but he rarely got a punch in. I'd find a wall and, with my back to it, duck and weave so fast that his fists would scrape brick till he bled.

Usually it was three or four against one. The worst part was waiting for the ambush. I could taste the blood in my mouth, feel the wind being kicked out of me. My attackers would huddle in the yard, metres from me, laughing as they planned their attack. Then they'd approach, slowly fanning out around me, encircling me with their hatred. Their scare tactics were pointless. They knew I wouldn't run, beg or cry. Accepting defeat would be like accepting their judgement of me, admitting that I was, somehow, less than them. I learnt to bury my fear, or at least to silence it.

Eventually the teacher on yard duty would tire of the spectacle and make a show of breaking up the fight. My attackers were told to wash their hands of my blood and I would be sent home in disgrace for again starting a fight. Occasionally, a group would follow me home. They liked to clean up after themselves.

'This will get the blood off your jumper,' they'd laugh,

as they threw me into the creek. On warm summer days I would hide in the forest until my clothes dried, feasting on blackberries. On wet winter days I dried off in our barn before returning home to Mamme. The bruises and cuts were harder to hide.

'Aaron, they'll kill him. Talk some sense into your son,' my mother would cry upon seeing me.

'This is not what I meant by being proud of your difference,' Tatte would preach. 'You can't talk these people out of hating you. Not with your words or with your fists. This is just the way it is here.'

My father would try to convince me that what mattered most was that I knew I deserved better treatment. I knew he was concerned for my safety. Still, no amount of schoolyard beatings or his reasoning could stop me. I was too hardheaded. I never asked for protection or called for help. Knowing that the school administration was in on it was terrifying. I still needed to know I could trust grown-ups. I wanted to believe that if I just waited, soon we'd all grow up—and out—of this meanness.

In the meantime, I would learn. My classmates could restrain me physically but they couldn't control my mind. That's where I had it over them. Knowledge was my way out of that town and, more than anything, I wanted out. Mr Lukac, my junior school teacher, a man of medium height, average build and sandy brown hair, is one of the few faces I can still bring sharply into focus. His kindness and attention allowed me to hope for a future and a life beyond the rutted dirt roads of Porubka. We talked of life on the outside. Of cities with paved roads and circuses, of distant countries and

Saturday: Jew-boy

professions open to me if I worked hard enough. He was a sad man and I came to understand that, although he wasn't Jewish, the mounting intolerance and hostile sentiment sweeping the school pained him, too. That he, an adult, was powerless to stop it was far more frightening than the beatings.

I studied hard, reading every page of my textbooks until I knew them off by heart. I never turned in unfinished homework and was the first to volunteer for any task. I loved learning. I liked being smart, smarter than the rest of them. Every 'A' grade I received took me ten steps further from my little hometown, to the city, where anyone could make it if they were intelligent and industrious enough. Somehow, I had come to believe that if I got far away enough, my life would be meaningful. Not that I knew what 'meaningful' was—I was just a kid, clinging to the belief that hatred and cruelty were the domain of the ignorant and uncultured. The city would be my salvation.

Not critical to this plan, but part of my necessary education, was religious studies. In those days there were no Jewish schools. Jewish children had to attend 'Cheder' after regular classes and on Sunday. We were the exception, with a live-in private tutor. Mr Wasserman was to ensure we were well versed in the Torah, fluent in Hebrew and painfully aware of the Ten Commandments. He received my bruises, cuts and swollen eyes with cold indifference.

'You are a Jew, Emil. A stranger in a strange land,' he would say, directing me to a prayer book. 'Only in the Promised Land will the beatings stop.'

We had a small house, but we had to make room for

the teacher to live, sleep and eat with us. Wasserman was a tall, enormously fat fellow who ate slowly but consumed an enormous amount. Food was scarce, so the more he ate, the less we had. I hated him, not only for the food he took from our mouths, but for the cruel and sadistic punishments he so enjoyed. Wasserman loved giving surprise tests, and if you got even one answer wrong, out came the cane. The fingers suffered first, with increasing incompetence attracting the back and then the bottom. Being struck wasn't the worst of it — I was no stranger to pain. What I hated was undressing and bending over, knowing that this man, a Jew, was enjoying it. My mother would bathe my hands in warm water and try to console me, but I knew there was nothing to be done about Wasserman. It wasn't easy to attract private tutors to a small village, and a cruel teacher was better than no teacher when it came to a Jewish education.

Still, even with the playground beatings and difficult religious instruction, I loved my religion. I couldn't wait until Saturday — a whole day to spend with Tatte in synagogue! Our Shul was always cold and the wooden bench seats hard, but I could sit there for hours. While father would concentrate more on his prayers than on me, at least I was with him. Sometimes Tatte would even draw me close and let me warm my hands in his pockets. On High Holy days he would smile at me, a lopsided half-smile, and call me by my pet name, 'Elyuka'. More usually, we would sit side by side, he rocking back and forth, lost in prayer, and I silent and still, feeling important just being near him.

Tatte was very religious. He prayed twice a day, observed the Sabbath, kept a kosher house and celebrated all religious holidays. We were expected to do the same. Like his father before him he was a pious, righteous man to whom charity was a way of life. I wanted to be just like him when I grew up.

My father was head of the Jewish community, as well as the Jewish communities in the surrounding villages. He was president of Porubka's only synagogue and therefore its congregation's leader. Our synagogue was a refuge, a place we Jews could band together and feel safe. It was where Jews came to talk to God and each other. As the closest rabbi was miles away, Tatte, being highly respected, became 'Mediator of Disputes'. Our community was of the old world, where the secular legal system ran second to religious decree, so Tatte's word was final. With that power came a strong sense of responsibility. Our district was one of the poorest in Czechoslovakia. We were poor, too, but we had shoes, so my father worked not only to support us, but also the district's poorer Jews.

I would trail Tatte as he walked from door to door, urging the wealthier of our community to give to those more needy. Half his income went to support a penniless, fatherless family of six. He was a serious, smart, spiritual man and we accepted his decisions without question, even when our stomachs rumbled with hunger or our shoes were worn through. I remember one winter, puzzling over the disappearance of my new woollen winter coat. I was distraught. My mother had saved all summer to purchase it. A week later, walking to school in last season's jacket, I saw it on the back of the milkman's son. My mother grabbed my hand as I lunged for the boy.

'Another gift from your father,' she whispered.

Tatte was also a busy man. Our time together was limited to the time it took to eat lunch. Mamme would bring our plates to the table, and Tatte would call us in, and invite us to talk. He asked only about our schoolwork, our lessons with Wasserman and our plans for the future. Sometimes he would talk of his own life, of the Great War and serving on the Italian front, and I would beg to see his right leg, scarred by a piece of flying shrapnel. But his monologue would not last long, because soon he'd be drawing parallels between life and the Torah's teachings, and inviting debate.

'Always think. Always question,' he would say, soaking up the remaining sauce on his plate with a piece of bread.

Tatte spent as much time away from home as in it. I got used to his absences. I didn't expect to be read to. I didn't hope to share jokes. I knew my father loved me and that he expected big things from me. I knew this because Mr Lukac had let slip that my father was saving for my university education. I pretended not to know, but I couldn't help blushing whenever I saw my father after that, and I swore to myself then that his money would not go to waste.

My father was a merchant who dealt in liquor, horses, farm produce and equipment. For three summers and autumns, he employed the district's peasants to collect weeds from the surrounding forests. I watched him negotiate, first with the peasants, then with the city men in fancy suits—men, he explained, who paid handsomely for the weeds. Men who would turn the weeds into medicine. He was a Jew, and loathed for it, but respected all the same. I saw how the peasants listened to him and how the men in suits shook his hand.

'My Tatte is smart,' I would boast to our goat, 'the smartest man in the whole world.'

When Tatte left Porubka on business, each absence felt like an eternity. He was a major presence in our family, even if not an altogether hands-on one.

Mamme, on the other hand, was a constant presence. Although managing our general store exhausted her, she would greet us after school, prepare dinner, help us with homework, and end each night with a story or a song. She sang of faraway places and happier times, and encouraged us to dream and believe in those dreams, even when it seemed our dreams were impossible. While Tatte was strict, my mother was soft and smiling and kind. She smelt of sweet tea and warm biscuits and although she had rough hands and wore a shopkeeper's apron and sensible shoes, I always thought of her as delicate.

My parents never argued. Whether that was because my mother never questioned my father, or because they had a true meeting of the minds, I'll never know. Either way, they were a good fit for each other. My mother's sweet, placid nature softened my father, and he looked after her most treasured possession—her family—well.

I knew my parents loved each other. Not from any outward expression of love—the ultra-orthodox were not permitted to touch or kiss in public. It was in the way they spoke to each other. When most of the town's women were being beaten weekly (our neighbour often came bleeding and bruised to our door), my father spoke to my mother only with kindness.

I loved spending time with Mamme, especially in our kitchen, which was filled with the warm and familiar smells of onion, cabbage and stewing meat. Every Sabbath, Mamme would let me knead the dough for our traditional bread (*challah*) and together we would walk down the main road to the communal oven, between the two rows of houses that made up our village, heaving the braided loaves—Mamme and her 'big, strong boy'. My mother was always affording me special treatment. I was pale and scrawny, unlike my siblings who were solid. This worked in my favour. Mamme was forever trying to fatten me up. I got used to reaching under the table towards her and taking a second, secret helping of beans or stew. I would wait until the others left the table, still whining about their empty bellies, and then run upstairs to devour my second helping, alone, in the attic.

But, for the most part, there was little I didn't share with my four siblings. We shared a bedroom, ate our meals together and bathed together. We stayed warm on winter nights by dragging our hay mattresses into the kitchen to sleep on the bare earth floor in front of the fire. Our home, a straw-topped, two-bedroom mud-brick house at the top of Porubka's only hill didn't allow us much privacy. Or luxury. We lived without running water, sewerage, gas or electricity. We drew our drinking water from one of the town's four wells. I had no toys. But it was a home filled with the smell of my mother's cooking, the noise of too many children and a sense of family.

We had a big family before the war. Rozsi, my eldest half-sister, lost her mother at birth. My father Aaron married my mother Fani two years later and soon added my two elder brothers Alex and Willie as well as my sister Cili to the brood. I was born on 10 September 1930. My mother told me that I walked early and talked early, ferociously imitating my siblings in a vain attempt to show the world that I was as smart and fast and strong as they were.

I had a grandfather, too—a thin, severe man with a long, white beard—and an uncle who had died in a farming accident and an aunt so sad that she had killed herself by jumping down a well. I had cousins—more than a dozen—some of them orphaned, others struggling to survive with only a mother to care for them. But they all lived in villages several hours' journey by horse and cart, so we rarely saw them.

By the time I was eight most of my brothers and sisters had left home. Rozsi went to live in the neighbouring city of Ungvar, where a wealthy uncle on her mother's side paid for her high-school education. Rozsi was a rarity in our town; unmarried at sixteen and studying at high school. My year revolved around religious holidays, when Rozsi would return home to visit. I would sit by her side, indulging her love of the limelight, and listen to her talk of high school, studying, sports and friendship. I could hardly wait for high school. Swimming in Rozsi's size-sixteen school jumper with one of Tatte's old ties knotted around my neck, I would chase her around the house, imitating the boys who chased her around the schoolyard, a scene that infuriated our father.

'It's not my fault I'm the best-looking girl in class,' Rozsi would laugh.

Over dinner, my chair pulled close to hers, I would ask

her, again, to walk me through the city. I would shut my eyes and follow her to Ungvar Castle, stopping to cool my feet in the shallows of the river Ung, bending to pick a lilac.

'Tell me again,' I would say, pulling at her skirt, 'about the costumes', and she would humour me, and for the third time that day, tell me about the spring festival. About the embroidered aprons in burnt oranges and bright reds, worn over petticoats and peasant skirts, and the market stalls and the smells and noises and people, so many people.

'Let's get out of here,' my big sister would say, and there was nothing to do but obey. Another one of her picnics, I'd lament, wishing that just one time, she was referring to Porubka. We picnicked every time Rozsi came to visit. Rozsi picked the trail into the forest and I packed the food. Most holidays the hamper was packed by the time Rozsi had bought her train ticket home.

I would sling a faded knapsack, heavy with cold meats, bread and fruit over my shoulder, Mamme's favourite kitchen knife tucked inside, and hop from rock to rock crossing streams behind my sister.

'Look, fish!' I yelled on one occasion, peering into a swirling stream and losing my balance. I yelled again, louder, as Mamme's sharpest knife tore into my thigh. In an instant, Rozsi was by my side, tearing the blade from my flesh, drying my tears and applying her headscarf as a tourniquet. Rozsi, who survived starvation and the tortures of concentration camp to be taken by cancer at sixty-two. I think of her every time I see my scar.

Then there was Alex, who wasn't afraid of anyone or anything. Not even Tatte, who was always telling him off for not praying enough, not studying enough or not spending enough time with family.

'Why do I pay for all these Hebrew lessons when you can't even obey the simplest of God's commandments—honour thy father and mother?' Tatte would ask.

When Alex was fifteen, he left for the city to be apprenticed as a merchant. Unlike his older sister he rarely came home, and chided father for giving his wages to the Jewish community instead of his family. My mother always came to Alex's defence, reasoning that he had to adapt his ways to the big city. She was sure that one day we would all be proud of him.

Willie, two years younger than Alex, was my friend and protector. When he left to be apprenticed in the city I felt lost. Willie taught me how to use my fists to defend myself and to harden my heart to hatred. Where my father taught me honesty and my mother taught me love, Willie taught me to laugh. Whether skimming stones across a creek to have fishermen believe a stream was teeming with fish, or tapping someone on the shoulder and running for cover, Willie made life into a game, one that I wanted to play. He was my hero and ultimately my saviour.

Cili was two years older than me and served as my second mother. Not because I needed one, but because she coveted the role. Cili looked as I imagine my mother would have when she first caught my father's eye—pale eyes, round face, creamy soft skin. Though Cili never chose the city over me, she worked long days in our general store, so that life, in a way, separated us, too.

And so, left for the most part alone and friendless, I learnt to amuse myself. I spent a lot of time outdoors with our animals. We had a horse for transportation, a cow for milk and a goat for company. I named them all and made them my friends—even the goat, who took a bit of convincing. I shared my fears and my future plans with them and not once did they laugh at me or tell me that my dreams were impossible.

Three

APRIL 1998

I was the youngest child, which meant I always wanted to be older, taller, stronger. I wished away time then. Now I want it back. All those times I could have sat at the kitchen table with my father for just a little longer, the offers to attend Red Cross meetings together or to join him canvassing for donations for Jewish Welfare, rebuffed for a night out with friends. All those times that I never had growing up. It was my mother who cut my toast into soldiers. Mum who taught me to tie my laces and who drove me to slumber parties. My mother who kept the pantry stocked with chocolate pudding and in whose wardrobe I sheltered from thunderstorms, comforted by her floor-length gowns and warm winter coats. My mother who bought me my first bra and kept my brothers out of my bedroom. Every day she would sit beside me at the piano and listen to me practise scales. It can't have been fun, but she never let on, never hinted that there was something else she'd rather be doing.

My mother stayed home while my father absented himself from lunchboxes, readers and science projects to meet with diamond suppliers, pearl threaders and jewellery-store owners. He couldn't pick me up from school because he was busy with bank managers. Dad made the sparkly jewellery and brought home the pocket money. My job was to bring home an 'A' on my social studies assignment. It was demanding work for both of us.

My father knew how to parent. When my eldest brother Peter was born, my father attacked parenthood like he would any new task: he raided the local bookshop and lined his bookshelf with self-help tomes entitled *How to be a Father* and *Your Child and the School*. He attended Parent Effectiveness Training programs and studied the Victorian Department of Health's childcare manual. He knew the theory; he just didn't have time to practise.

So I saved up the school news, sports news, test results and gossip for dinner-time. Dad always showed up for dinner. The television was turned off, the radio turned down and newspapers filed away. Meal time was sacred in our family—and noisy. Wedged in beside my father at the head of the table, I had to struggle to be heard. There was the clatter of dishes, pleas for more apricot chicken, and always the more important, more interesting information my brothers had to offer. It was hard to show off my mastery of the ABC when my older brothers were conjugating verbs.

And when my father did have time, he liked to do boy stuff with my brothers—climb trees, arm-wrestle, build forts. I didn't mind the odd water-pistol fight but if surrendering my crayons and hairclips was a prerequisite to spending time with my father, I just couldn't do it. I found other ways to get his attention. Dad liked brains. I saw how he smiled his lopsided half-smile whenever Gary or Peter brought home good grades, how his chest puffed up when his boys were named school captains. So I did the same, drawing him out of his study to show off my report cards and by wearing my school captain and sports captain badges—anything to prove his daughter was as smart and successful as her brothers, and equally deserving of his attention. I studied around the clock for my high-school certificate, not to secure a place at Melbourne University, but to beat my brothers' impressive results.

I knew my father loved me as much as he loved my brothers. I was his 'little piece of pineapple', the 'apple of his eye'. I just wasn't a boy. As a teenager that meant having to be home by midnight while my brother Gary was without a curfew. It meant tears when I was discovered in the rumpus room at eighteen, kissing a boy, but congratulatory back-slapping when Peter lost his virginity at sixteen. It meant not being asked my opinion. It hurt. I wanted my father to take me seriously. I wanted not just his love, but his respect. I thought a job with a big-name city law firm was what he would want for me.

In Fiji, I listen to my father talk with reverence about his Tatte, the community leader, the provider, the giver—often absent, always achieving—and his Mamme, soft and innocent, the one who tucked them in at night, and suddenly our home life makes sense. I listen as my father talks of the weight of his father's expectations and his need, so strong, to see that lopsided grin, to have just a slice of his Tatte's attention, to be as good and wise and strong as his old man, and I laugh.

Four

SUNDAY: CATTLE TRAINS

I was eight when the German army rolled into Czechoslovakia. We didn't have a radio, or money for newspapers, so 15 March 1939 passed as just another unremarkable day in my ninth year of life. Even if my father, on his travels, had brought home news of the Occupation I doubt I'd have paid attention. Porubka had been preoccupied with Aryan supremacy for years. How much worse could the Nazis be?

When I was eleven, Nazi Germany gifted the eastern part of Czechoslovakia, including Porubka, to Hungary as a reward for its friendship and cooperation. The Hungarians forced us to wear armbands with the Star of David tacked onto them. I watched my mother silently cut a length of canary yellow cloth into three perfect stars, then stitch them onto three loops of black elastic. She slipped an armband over my shirtsleeve, drew me close and whispered, 'Wear it every day, Emil, promise me.'

Sunday: Cattle Trains

My mother looked tired and, for the first time, scared. I promised.

I soon learnt why Mamme feared the armband. If you were caught without it, the police, the military, even an enraged citizen, was entitled to beat you for flouting the law. And if you did wear it, well, anything you got was deserved.

The Hungarian soldiers who had flooded in by the hundreds were brutal to the Jews and the Slovaks, and even to their own. The first time I saw Hungarian officers stringing up a fellow soldier I stopped in disbelief to watch. The soldier, who looked to be still in his teens, winced as his superiors wound a length of rope around his wrists. I watched as the soldier was guided up a ladder, his arms drawn up and the rope flung over a tree branch and knotted twice. I heard the sickening snap of dislocated shoulders, but resisted the urge to run to the hanging boy. As the soldier's superiors turned to leave, I saw one of them laugh. I ran around the corner and threw up. Two hours later, returning home, I turned my head from the scene, but not before noticing the same baby-faced soldier, now unconscious, still swinging from the branch.

It wasn't that I felt sorry for the hanging soldier. On some level I felt relief—every arm dislocated was one arm less capable of beating me. It was just that I was scared: if these men enjoyed watching each other suffer, torturing us Jews would be bliss. As I walked the streets past uniforms of green and black, my yellow star blazing on my arm, I wished I were invisible.

I avoided the beatings but couldn't ignore the violence around me. Jews, gypsies, and the politically questionable were regularly beaten, most commonly with rifle butts, occasionally with the gloved hand of a German or Hungarian officer. At eleven, my thoughts should have been of school, girls and sports. Instead, all I thought about was staying alive, so I stopped roaming the village and spent more time at home.

When my parents talked of Hitler or the Nazi party they spoke in Hungarian so that I wouldn't understand. I was curious about their conversations but never asked father to translate. I was living the war and things were getting worse. I didn't need confirmation.

One night my father returned home late, distressed, his eyes swollen and red. I'd never seen Tatte shaken. It scared me. He sat on his bed, head bowed, and told my mother of the fate of their good friend Jacob. I hadn't consciously set out to learn Hungarian but somehow over the years I'd picked up just enough of the language to decipher my father's report: his oldest friend had been beaten to death by Hungarian officers for having been outdoors five minutes after curfew.

I wasn't allowed onto the front lawn past dusk after that. I didn't resist. I was tired of sidestepping trouble. My high-school classmates had become bolder, buoyed by the increase in number of their anti-Jewish supporters. They would yell abuse, steal my lunch and attack me in the hallways, knowing our teachers would feign ignorance. Saturday mornings were the worst: the dusty track to the synagogue would be lined with families spitting, cursing and hurling stones at us.

To prove their loyalty to Hitler, the Hungarians established a youth movement called 'Levente', the Hungarian version of the 'Hitler Youth', with the same purpose of training boys between the ages of twelve and eighteen in the ways of war. Attendance was compulsory and training took place on Mondays, Wednesdays and Thursdays after school. Children were taught to shoot, wrestle and throw grenades. They marched for Nazi world domination. Hitler was their friend.

I'd been naïve enough to believe that my services would be required. I didn't realise that when the call went out to every able-bodied man and woman to help in the war effort, Jews, gypsies and homosexuals were not included. I didn't realise we were the enemy. We were separated—trainees to the gun range, Jews to the toilet block. While the rest of the class learnt to load a gun, I collected rubbish and emptied the toilet pans. I became an even bigger joke in class. Now 'shit-cleaner' was added to my roll-call of names.

Although my early years were characterised by isolation and unkindness, somehow I never quite lost sight of who I was and what I wanted. My mother's love and my father's constant reassurances that things would return to normal allowed me to believe that one day I would turn my dream of escaping Porubka into a reality. Besides, it was easier to ignore the whispers about forced deportations and labour camps than to accept them.

My dream was helped along by the fact that my parents had miraculously convinced Mamme's sister in New York to take me in. The Aunt Merele of my imagination was a society dame, dripping with diamonds and swathed in silk. She was freedom, knowledge, friendship and plenty. As it turned out,

Aunt Merele was a worn-out, slightly depressed widow who was struggling to adapt to a strange new life, and barely able to pay the rent on her one-bedroom apartment. Aunt Merele came all the way to Porubka to collect me. But upon hearing whispers that the Hungarian authorities were making moves to nullify her American citizenship, she booked herself a return fare, sparing one of us the Holocaust experience.

'You understand, darling,' she said cupping my face in her cold, wrinkled hands, 'you're just too risky.'

In the midst of all this cruelty, I celebrated my Bar Mitzvah in September 1943. I had prepared for my passage to manhood for months, revising and perfecting the portion of the bible story I was to sing at synagogue on my thirteenth birthday. It was a big day for me, not because I felt any special affinity with God, but because it was my one chance to show my father that the trust and faith he'd put in me by saving up for my education were warranted. I wanted to make him proud.

A week before my birthday Tatte took me to Ungvar to be fitted for new trousers and a shirt. I pulled on my old trousers, worn through at the knees, and a frayed, white shirt, and pulled myself onto Tatte's work-cart, to sit beside him. Bessa's reigns lay slack on the bench seat between us.

'Noooo,' my father said, picking up the reins and handing them to me. 'If you want those pants we'd better get moving.'

I'd never been allowed to take the reins before. I grabbed them from Tatte's hands and, before he could change his mind, gave a yell and a heave and we were flying. I was going to like being thirteen.

Sunday: Cattle Trains

After a time, Tatte closed his eyes and asked me to sing my Bar Mitzvah portion—just as I'd sing it for the congregation the following week. I sang the first prayer, my voice shaky, and then my father smiled, so I sang some more, louder now. I sang all the way to Ungvar. And four hours later, a brown paper package resting between us, we rode home in silence, both of us deep in thought. My head was buzzing with all that I had seen—the mountains of cloth and tubs of buttons; the timber yards and salt factory; the yeshivahs and synagogue; and the Castle, imposing and elegant. I had seen what was possible and I'd seen it with Tatte.

I don't remember much of my actual birthday. I don't recall unwrapping presents, drinking a toast or dancing late into the night, but I do recall that I sat next to my father and two brothers in Shul. If that synagogue was still standing today I could go straight to our seats, perhaps because it was one of the few good memories I have of my early life, of feeling safe and secure and loved.

It was a particularly crowded Saturday. In the front row centre was my beaming Tatte. Alex and Willie sat on his left; I was on his right. As I approached the podium to take over the Torah reading I looked back at Alex smiling up at me, Willie winking, and my father flushed with pride. And on the balcony were the women in their synagogue finery, my mother blushing with excitement, Rozsi blowing me a kiss and Cili scanning the men's section for eligible suitors. I sang from the Torah, from memory, the words on the parchment dancing in front of me. I was now thirteen, and a man before God and my father. After I'd completed my recitation, I returned to my seat.

My father drew me into him and whispered in my ear: 'Elyuka, you've done well. Know, now, that if you put your mind to something, you will succeed. Whatever you strive for, you can achieve.'

❁

Within a few months of my Bar Mitzvah, Rozsi and Willie were visiting again, this time by order of the Hungarian authorities. Alex didn't return with them, choosing instead to ignore the ruling that unmarried Jewish persons return home to their parents. I was ecstatic. I'd missed them and had grown restless, confined at home without company.

Rozsi was now twenty-two and of marriageable age, if not disposition. My parents busied themselves and ignored the impending round-up and deportation of Jews by interviewing potential husbands for her. As it turned out, the war happened and Rozsi was spared an arranged marriage, and my parents denied the privilege of seeing her marry.

My parents' conversations were now, more often than not, spoken in whispers. I thought they spoke of prospective suitors, but perhaps they spoke of their fears for their children and the possibility of losing each other and everything to Hitler. Whatever their reality, they tried to protect us by altering ours. We were told life must go on as usual. Our studies mustn't suffer, and the chores still needed doing. Weathering the escalating violence was just another unpleasant thing we had to do. Even when word came that Alex had been hauled to a labour camp on the Russian front, my parents, with dry eyes, convinced us to forge on. Nothing would happen to us.

Sunday: Cattle Trains

In March 1944 something did happen. I woke before the sun rose to the sound of fists pounding at our front door. I hid in my bedroom and peered out at the two officers standing in the hallway. One of them forced something into my father's hand. Tatte, silent and unsmiling, waited for them to leave.

I ran from my room.

'What is it, Tatte? Is it about Alex?' I watched as he slowly unfolded a piece of paper. His face was so sad. Finally, he answered.

'It's an order, Elyuka. From the Hungarian Military Command. We must meet outside the synagogue tomorrow at 8.00 a.m. We are going on a trip. Now, go and pack. *Go.*'

Father had called me Elyuka. We weren't at the synagogue and I hadn't done anything worthy of praise. Something bad was about to happen.

Mamme spent the next twenty-four hours cramming blankets, towels, crockery and underwear into bags as father rocked incessantly, lost in feverish prayer. I don't know whether they considered running or hiding, but I doubt it. Porubka was too small and our friends too few to realistically entertain a successful subterfuge.

I spent that evening with Rozsi and Willie in our room, trying to guess our destination. Were we being sent to the city to work or to join other Jews from neighbouring towns in one of the ghettos we'd heard about? I fell asleep late and woke before dawn. In the half-light I could make out Mamme, still sorting and repacking. Now she was adding plum jam, bread and sliced veal to our bags. Tatte had promised I'd only miss a few days of school, but I began to have doubts. I approached him, interrupting his prayers. Hunched on a wooden chair, in his dark-grey suit and with only his curly black hair and hat visible above his prayer book, Tatte looked up.

'What about the goat, Tatte? Who will feed him?' I asked.

Tatte smiled his lopsided half-smile, but did not answer.

I soon forgot about our goat when, rounding the corner to the synagogue, I saw our town square swarming with people. Soldiers in black SS uniforms hustled families along, prodding at the elderly with their rifles. A line had formed, snaking its way towards three huge open-air trucks. Children grabbed at their mother's skirts and men dragged bags overflowing with clothing, food and prayer books. Officers were shouting, babies were crying and mothers begged their children to stay close. Mostly there was bewilderment and fear. I reached for my mother's hand and, looking up at her, caught her wiping away tears.

I lied to her for the first time. 'Don't be sad, Mamme. It will be fun on the truck.'

It took less than two hours to load the dozens of bags and unwilling passengers onto the trucks. Six hours later, we arrived at the Ungvar Brick and Tile Factory to join thousands of others in what was to be our home for the next three weeks. Willie scouted around and found a disused brick kiln in which to make our beds. We smoothed a rug to soften the cement floor and lay down, covering ourselves with our warm, woollen blankets, which still smelled of home. We knew we were the lucky ones. Most people hadn't thought to pack bedding, and due to lack of space were forced to sleep outdoors on frozen ground. Huddling together, we kept each other a little warmer than we otherwise would have been, thankful for the protection from the wind and driving rain.

I woke on our first night to hear my parents talking. They must have thought I was asleep, and had dispensed with second languages to conceal their conversation.

'Aaron, these people are animals. Look at my children shivering. I've no mittens for them. They'll freeze to ...'

Father put a finger to her lips. 'Hush, Fani. God will look after us. Our children are his children.'

I rolled over and shifted under my blanket. I didn't want to hear of my parents' fears; my movement, calculated to attract their attention, worked to silence them. It was a horrible realisation, knowing my mother was frightened, that we were all in danger, and that maybe my parents knew more than they were letting on. I tried to return to the fog of sleep, to blissful ignorance and false hope, but it was too late. The following day and the days after that, father tried to reassure us that our dwelling was only temporary and that soon we would be set free, but his words were hollow and failed to comfort me. I cried every time I saw Mamme cry. I may have been thirteen, but I didn't feel like a man.

Life in the brick factory was miserable. It was filthy, muddy, wet and cold, and we spent most of our days queuing up for the latrines as our stomachs adjusted to our new diet. I was terribly hungry. We'd rationed our food, but divided by six, it hadn't lasted more than seven days. There was no more buttered bread or plum jam, and my stomach churned, crying out for more than the stale crusts and dirty water doled out to us. On especially cold nights my mother would cover me with her skirt to stop my teeth from chattering.

Mostly I remember spending my days wandering around the factory, stopping at a cluster of men or a group of boys debating their future. Everyone had a theory. I hoped we were being transported to Poland or Germany to work in factories. I knew we weren't going home.

My father dismissed my theory. 'What nonsense. Why would they take small children and the elderly, then?'

The real answer was so horrific it was beyond a god-fearing man like my father to contemplate.

After three weeks at Ungvar we were told to pack our bags. We were to assemble at the train station and leave our luggage on the platform. I stepped into a queue behind my father and inched forward slowly, past carriages with leather upholstery and cargo wagons bulging with army supplies. I stopped at the mouth of a cattle train and faltered, confused, but the swell of the line carried me up and in, after my parents. The door was bolted behind us. It was pitch black. There must have been ninety of us in there, side by side, heads tilted to the roof, straining upwards for the little fresh air that seeped through the slats. Within minutes people collapsed, becoming makeshift cushions for those still upright. I could hear my father praying but Mamme was silent. No more songs of better times or faraway places.

We stopped and started, lurched and fell as our train made way for the more important troop-carrying carriages. Our door remained locked for seventy-two hours, without food, water or toilet stops. We survived on the crumbs in our pockets and relieved ourselves where we stood. A metal dish had been placed on the floor in the centre of the carriage at the beginning of our journey. The makeshift toilet pan soon overflowed and was shifted to a corner where it festered for three days. The stench in the cabin was unbearable — a mixture of urine, faeces, vomit and dead bodies.

It was hard to differentiate day from night but exhaustion brought on sleep. I woke every few hours to the bickering of my neighbours. Misha was breathing too much air, Hershey took up too much space and Marika wasn't sharing her food. By the second day the carriage had grown quiet. People were too weak and dejected to argue. I spent the first day with my family reminiscing about the past and questioning the future; but as the hours passed and our futures grew bleaker, we, too, talked less. Soon all I could hear was the clunk of the wheels and my father's whispered prayers. I prayed, too, for someone to hear him.

The silence was occasionally broken by loud sobs and every so often by Yankel, one of Porubka's better-known bachelors. Driven mad by the depravity, he'd started to talk of an imaginary wife and child. It stung to hear him give religious instruction to his little boy and beg his wife to come to bed but I hadn't the energy or inclination to comfort him.

I had my own problems. Willie had secured a dead body for me to lie on and someone was moving in on my territory. I grappled around in the dark and shoved the intruder in the head. I didn't know if the corpse I lay on was male or female, stranger or family friend, and I didn't care. The body was softer than the floor, I was tired and my instinct to survive was winning in the battle for my conscience. I stretched out and slept.

Three days after setting off, we stopped and the carriage doors were flung open. I had longed for the sun, but after seventy-two hours in the dark, the light stabbed at my eyes. It was cold outside but the rush of clean air was a relief. I was too weak and numb to step off the train so my father helped me to my feet and lifted me off, steadying me on the platform. Officers brushed past us, dragging the dead after them, piling them on top of one another. Babies, old women, teenage boys, all in a heap. And then live ones — children too weak to walk, grandmothers too frail to stand — were loaded onto barrows and carted away. Piled one on top of the other by German officers with their heads held high.

Five

MAY 1998

I'd never seen my father cry until one day in his study, when his family's grief got the better of him. Under different circumstances, at a different time, the sight would have devastated me. My father had always been, or at least always seemed, invincible. I'd never seen him inactive, apathetic or suffering self-doubt. Dad was always moving forward.

'If you're going to do something,' my parents used to say, 'do it with a smile.'

So I smiled. That's what Brauns did. We smiled. We weren't angry or frustrated or melancholy. We solved our problems and moved on. It helped that we weren't wired to be moody or needy or prone to moments of depression. Sometimes I wished I were more melodramatic, more passionate about the things I enjoyed, less controlled. I wondered what it would be like *not* to be sunny.

I looked at my father, my new, sick father. A father who shared his feelings, a father who cried. Not because he felt sorry for himself, but because he had forced his children to confront mortality. I hadn't come that far. I was still about keeping it together and keeping a secret. At the age of thirty-two, my father's dying was the first bad thing that had ever happened to me and I didn't know how to talk about it. I was uneasy in the spotlight, with being the person other people felt sorry for. I wasn't practised at being vulnerable. I didn't know how to accept sympathy.

It took me four weeks to tell my best friend that my father was dying. It was easier than I thought, and the telling helped. And the little opening that I'd fashioned for my friends opened them up to me. It was as though by admitting my life was no longer perfect, I was permitting my friends their imperfections. Because I was allowing them to judge me they no longer felt judged by me. In accepting comfort I was accepting their friendship. I wondered how Dad's friendships had fared.

'Some have disappointed me: the ones who think that by not mentioning the illness it will go away. The ones who never visit because they can't get past their own fears and insecurities about old age and illness. I know it's hard and that they don't mean anything by it, but I miss them. Mostly, the friendships are stronger. People whom I rarely saw make time for me now. They want to be a part of this and live through it, and learn from it, with me. It feels good to let them.'

The first time I tried a vitamin supplement I was twenty-five. I had a raging cold sore and a date on Saturday night. My sister-in-law Lesley, a naturopath, suggested a herbal remedy. I was sceptical. We did drugs in our family if a doctor prescribed them, but we never touched herbs. My father never saw the point in it.

'Why take vitamin C when you can suck an orange?' he once said in response to a childhood request for the little orange lollies.

For Dad there was no alternative; there *was* only Western medicine.

But Western medicine had failed him. It had thrown up its hands and walked away. Now he was willing to believe in alternative therapies, in the possibility of miracles, in the existence of men and women with the power to heal, and he set about looking for them.

He filled his days with friends, family and physiotherapy, but he also tried kinesiology and Chinese medicine. He let people run their hands over his body to redistribute his energy. He tried acupuncture and acupressure. He withstood manipulation and massage and heated suction cups. He listened as one practitioner after another told him it was his back, his shoulders and his liver that were to blame. He swallowed handpicked herbs and drank foul-smelling potions. He listened to soothing music and joined in rhythmic chants. He closed his eyes and concentrated on expelling his disease.

He did it because he had no alternative.

Six

MONDAY: A7639

The sign at the station read 'Birkenau' in big, bold letters. I'd never been to a funeral before, never seen a dead person up close. And here they were on platform five, bodies piled five deep, limbs disjointed, eyes empty. Everywhere, death. A prisoner brushed past me, dragging a corpse. He stopped to readjust his grip on the dead man's ankles and then walked on towards the mountain of dead at the end of the platform. A young boy chased after the body, crying, 'Grandpa, grandpa get up.'

I stuck close to Tatte as we were led through a sea of uniforms: Gestapo wore green, SS wore black, and prisoners wore blue and white. The Jews had a yellow star tacked onto their striped pyjamas. Prisoners busied themselves separating the dead from the living.

We were directed to form two lines. 'Men to the right. Women, children and the elderly to the left!'

Tatte let go of my hand. He kissed my sisters, hugged me to his chest and then kissed Mamme before the two were pulled apart by an impatient SS officer. Separated from Tatte, I drifted to the left with my mother and sisters when a Jewish prisoner in his twenties pulled me from the queue.

'Where's your father?' he asked in Yiddish. I motioned towards Tatte.

'Go to him,' the young man whispered. 'Stand on his feet—you'll look taller. Hurry now, the inspection is about to begin.'

I ran after my father and repeated what I'd heard.

'I think we should trust him, Elyuka,' my father instructed. 'He risked his life to speak to you.'

My father took my hand and I steadied myself, one foot on his shoe, one on Willie's. The guards made a cursory tour of the men's group and I passed first inspection. We were instructed to walk on. Up ahead we saw a committee of officers standing on a podium. The prisoners who passed in front of the podium were stopped by the officers and inspected for age, strength and health, and then sent on, or directed to the left to rejoin the women and children. One man in particular appeared to be in charge of the selection process. The other officers called him Dr Mengele. I would later hear him referred to as 'The Angel of Death'.

'Willie, you go through first,' my father whispered. He turned to me, 'Emil, when Willie reaches the other side run to him as fast as you can. Don't stop moving until you're lost in the crowd on the other side. Okay?'

Willie approached the selection committee. Dr Mengele looked down at my brother, paused and then sent him to the right. It was my turn. I took one step, then another, and then I ran. Past the podium, past the officers and past an open-mouthed Dr Mengele, who shouted, 'Stop Jew, get back here, you dog.'

But I kept running. Running until I was buried in the crush of men I later discovered were to be selected for survival.

A guard grabbed my father. 'You were next in line. Go get your son,' the man instructed, pointing his weapon at my father's head.

'What son? I'm a bachelor. I have no wife and children,' my father replied, his voice assured.

'Then *we'll* find him and shoot the both of you,' the guard said, shoving my father into the group in which I stood. I held my breath. Tatte remained resolute and the interrogation wore on. Fortunately the argument began to bore the guard and he dispensed with his questioning and left for more interesting game. Tatte waited ten minutes before coming to find me. I knew not to hug him.

We were herded into an enormous barrack and ordered to undress, remove our skullcaps and wait for a signal to proceed to the shower block.

I unbuttoned my crumpled shirt, slipped out of my Bar Mitzvah trousers, shed my underwear and stood next to Willie. I couldn't look at him. Not because I was embarrassed by his nakedness, but because Willie had always been unique in my eyes and it frightened me to see him stripped of his individuality, to see him part of a silent, shivering herd of men, flanked by guards carrying machine guns.

We wandered out to the shower block in single file.

'I'm not going. I won't,' threatened a skinny, pale boy two down from me in the queue. The guards heard him and took

Monday: A7639

aim, bringing him down with their first bullet. Gunfire spray brought down the next three in line.

I kept moving. A guard at the entrance to the shower block poked at my ribs with his rifle, his dog sniffed at my ankles.

'Get in, you filthy animal.'

I stepped onto the cold concrete floor next to my father. Eventually the water came and I drank. I turned my open mouth up to the huge shower rose and gulped at the icy water, scrubbing the dirt from my face and rubbing my cold, flat stomach. We were led outside, naked, cold and wet to drip-dry in the dusty grey square.

I was dunked in chemically treated water and shaved. Apart from my thick head of hair I was hairless, so the guard's razor was fast. I was almost glad when Tatte covered his nakedness with a prison uniform. He had looked alien, with his head shorn, his once soft downy chest and woolly arms now pale and smooth. I dressed quickly in oversized drawstring pants, a flimsy blue-and-white striped jacket and hard, wooden clogs. No underwear, socks, woollen gloves or winter coat, despite the cold.

I was ordered with father and Willie onto another convoy of trucks. This time we could see out and we watched the passing countryside, hypnotised by the spirals of black smoke rising from the chimneys of distant factories, sickened by the powerful, strange smell.

It was late afternoon by the time we were shown to our barrack. Father, Willie and I were assigned bunks on top of each other. We were each issued an aluminium dish and spoon, and served our first meal in three-and-a-half days — a slice of stale bread and green soup. I gagged on the food but forced it down. A prisoner, unidentifiable from the rest of us except for a smug attitude and whip, entered our barrack. He welcomed us to 'Auschwitz' and introduced himself as our Block Leader ('Kapo').

He explained the ground rules. 'If you lose your plate and spoon you don't get fed. If you question me or oppose me you won't be here tomorrow.'

As a welcoming gesture on our first night, our Kapo beat a man to death for speaking out of turn. We were forced to watch in silence, aware that if we were caught shifting uneasily or averting our eyes we would be next. I learnt to keep very quiet and still, when all I wanted to do was cry and scream and run.

I did cry, every night, once the lights were out. I was hungry and scared and cried out for Mamme. I missed her smile. I didn't talk to Tatte about my loneliness. I knew it would make him sad to think of her, and to think of me missing her. I never figured *he* might want a hug; he seemed consoled by God.

'God willing, we will all be reunited after the war,' he would say. His words held no comfort. I didn't think God was willing.

The next day we were in line again. A uniformed guard grabbed me, pushed me into a chair and pinned my wrists to the armrests while another guard stabbed at my forearm with a needle. Over and over again the needle pierced skin until, beneath the blood, I could make out a number in black ink.

'A7639, you're done.'

A bloodied rag was wiped across my arm. I looked at the

number. I had become a number. Not a person. Not even a Jew. Just a number. Save for my family, I would not be referred to by name again until liberation.

Years later, tired of recounting my wartime experience, I decided to have the tattoo removed. Dave, the tattoo artist, warned it would be difficult.

'Must have hurt like hell. Bloody unprofessional, going in that deep,' Dave said, by way of apology.

The third time I went to see Dave, he gave up.

'These are your choices,' he said. 'You can either pay a plastic surgeon to do a skin graft or I can cover your number up with another tattoo. I suggest the cheaper option,' Dave said, passing me a sketchbook of skeletons and Harley-riding hula girls. I flicked through the drawings.

'None of these designs appeal to me,' I said, reaching for the notepad and pen on Dave's desk.

I covered a few pages with swirls and doodles, finally settling on my fourth attempt. 'Can you do this?' I asked, pointing to a simple floral design, attracted to its serenity and modesty.

'No problem, mate,' Dave assured me.

Except he did too good a job. Everyone noticed my new tattoo. Now I had two stories to tell.

Our next home was a coal mine twelve kilometres from Auschwitz. Stepping off the truck I scanned my surroundings. 'Jawischowitz' comprised corrugated-iron barracks, a watchtower, curling barbed wire, and hard, grey earth. No grass, no trees, just a slew of guards. A tall, thin-lipped officer hurried past us, handing out plates and spoons. Another, pale and sullen and carrying a hessian sack, dispensed underwear and caps. I accepted a pair of musty underpants and a striped cap, and crammed them into my pocket.

Having completed a task he clearly despised, the second guard, looking even more put out, returned to me. As if to say 'it's all your fault', he grabbed my arm and wordlessly motioned for me to stand to one side, apart from the others. Father and Willie were, by now, being led away and I started after them, yelling, 'Don't leave me, Tatte … wait!' But I was held back by the guard, who propelled me in the opposite direction. I was led to a barrack, allocated a bunk and told to wait inside. Three hours later the door was flung open and sixty young men poured in.

'Welcome to the youth barracks! You really are young, aren't you?' said a boy who looked a lot older than Willie. 'I'm Andor,' he continued, throwing off his clogs and collapsing onto the bunk nearest mine, 'and I'm twenty. Lied about my age to get in here. You should see the other barracks. If you had, maybe you'd be smiling right now instead of looking so miserable.'

Andor was Slovak, from Kosice. He was a big talker, but kind and brave, and seeing that, at thirteen, I was years younger than the rest of them, took me under his wing. Andor explained that our barrack was the showpiece of the camp and much less crowded than the others. I was sad to hear that father and Willie shared a barrack with two hundred men, sleeping in three-tiered bunk-beds.

Andor showed me how to trade soup for bread, where to

wash and dry my one pair of underpants, and how to visit my father and Willie. Walking around the camp was forbidden, as was talking while in the food or toilet queues or at roll-call. Hunger and fatigue made dying easy here. I wasn't going to help death along by breaking the rules. Andor was fearless ... or stupid. He slipped in and out of lines of men marching from barracks to breakfast or roll-call to latrine, snaking his way closer to his sick father's barrack and slipping inside when the guards' backs were turned. He crept into the kitchen and stuffed his pants with scraps from the chopping blocks to share with his friends. He was beaten regularly.

I hated to watch and would beg him to be good. 'I'd rather see you alive than share another stolen meal with you!'

But Andor wouldn't listen. One night, after silently waving me goodbye from his bunk, Andor slipped out the door for a late-night visit to his father. He never returned.

I had little contact with Willie and father. During the day they were put to work underground shovelling coal, while I toiled above ground sorting the stones from the coal that emerged from the mines. Very occasionally I would sneak to their barrack at night for a few whispered words and the reassurance that they were still alive, timing my visits with the changing shifts of the guards. More often, Willie came to me. Though I ached to see him I was embarrassed by the comparative comfort of my surroundings, and worried that his visits would end as Andor's had, so I didn't encourage him to return.

Instead, I looked for my father and Willie in the latrine line, in the queue outside the kitchen and at roll-call. My father never spoke to me, but he'd fix his eyes on me and stare so intently that, coming away from roll-call, I'd feel like we'd shared a conversation. Sometimes he'd blink at me and I came to understand that this exaggerated blink was his way of telling me he loved me. It also spoke of deep sadness. Though I'd reply to his blink with a smile, Tatte never smiled back.

I thought less and less about my mother and sisters. I was too hungry, frightened and weak to think beyond my own survival. Occasionally I would wake from a dream, wondering about Mamme, and chide myself for being so self-absorbed. But then I would go to work, and my thoughts would fall away, and all I could see was the conveyer belt in front of me, and all I cared about was distinguishing stone from coal. I forced myself to concentrate, and willed myself to stay awake.

My workmate Isaac wasn't as focused and, one day, while cleaning our section of the belt, he allowed his mind to wander. His cloth got jammed in the cogs of the belt, and he yelled this awful pained cry, and tried to yank it out. That was when his arm went in after the cloth. It all happened so fast. Isaac yelled and I rushed to the motor to turn it off, but I was too late. Ripped clean from his shoulder, his arm was left dangling from the cogs. They carried Isaac away, blacked out and bleeding, in a half-filled wheelbarrow. I was assigned a new partner the next day. I didn't ask him his name.

The day of the accident, a Polish woman whose job it was to feed the guards stopped momentarily beside me.

'Life's cheap,' she said, struggling beneath a huge silver tray heaped with sandwiches. 'Don't expect to see your friend again.'

Monday: A7639

Her words were not spoken in anger, but rather as a warning.

The next day she passed even closer. 'Be under the belt in five minutes,' she whispered.

Without hesitating I slipped below the belt. A few minutes later a pair of clogs shuffled past, then stopped. A hand reached down, unfurled, and a shiny, whole, red apple dropped to the ground in front of me. I grabbed it, taking urgent, greedy bites, wondering what I'd done to deserve such kindness. Every day after that, I ate hurriedly under the churning wheels of the conveyor belt. Fresh rye bread, pears, pickles—whatever the guards had discarded or left untouched. Some days, my Polish friend, Zosia, would join me in my secret restaurant, and I would talk of home-cooked meals and baking *challah* with Mamme. Zosia rarely talked, except to enquire if the bread was still fresh and the coffee warm. When I left Jawischowitz suddenly, six months later, I didn't get to say goodbye.

I made other friends. I quickly learnt that although I was responsible for my own survival, I craved companionship. Socialising wasn't permitted, so most conversations were whispered. Proximity encouraged friendship, and I became close to the boys who slept beside, above and below me. Joseph slept on my right. He had pale skin, intelligent eyes and a photographic memory. He preferred bible study to coal-mining. Each Monday Joseph would complain to the Kapo of a different malady, rubbing the Kapo's thermometer under his blanket until his temperature soared.

I'd beg Joseph to be more careful, warning that his constant complaints would eventually arouse suspicion. But he laughed me off. 'When I'm sick in bed, I have the whole day to pray to God. He won't let anything happen to me!'

Three weeks after we met, Joseph was taken away. Rumour had it that a German doctor had come to the youth barrack during the day for a surprise inspection. Minutes earlier Joseph had turned in a thermometer reading of 39.5 degrees. The doctor took Joseph's pulse and then his temperature, not leaving his bedside until he'd retrieved the instrument which indicated a temperature of 36.5 degrees. I never saw Joseph again.

One by one my friends disappeared: Jacob, the religious scholar turned cynic whose faith in God wilted with the insurgence of the Nazi party; Pali, the doctor's son who cried for his maid; and Eli, the youngest of eleven very poor children who, accustomed to an empty stomach and second hand clothes, never complained. Our friendships were built on trust and loyalty. We guarded each other's possessions and nursed each other through illness. Practising kindness helped us retain our humanity.

I could be heartless when I had to be. I stole food once from a dead boy, Vasil, a Russian two bunks up from me. I knew from watching him that he had food piled under his mattress: week-old bread, mouldy vegetables, withered apple cores. I'd seen him slip his breakfast under his bunk each time he was too sick to eat. One morning when I woke, I noticed Vasil lying motionless on his bed. I called out to him, but he didn't answer. I ran to his bunk and shook him. He was dead. By roll-call his body would be disposed of, and by noon his bunk would be stripped. I reached under his bunk, gathered his provisions, and slid them under my mattress.

Monday: A7639

To ease my guilt, I distracted myself by writing. I lay on the floor and etched an imaginary diary entry into the dust. I hadn't touched a pencil in months. I wrote three lines and signed my name—my real name, heartened that I could still write and spell, even if it was finger-painting. It reminded me of doing homework for Wasserman. I re-read my words:

Today I stole from a dead boy. His food would have gone to waste if I hadn't and Mamme hates waste. I'm glad Mamme's not here. She'd hate to see me so skinny.

I turned fourteen in Jawischowitz. I know this because after roll-call one day my father stepped away from his line and walked towards me. Drawing me to him I saw the hint of a smile, an echo of his lopsided grin.

'Happy birthday, Elyuka,' he whispered, kissing my sunken cheeks. And then he was gone, back among his spindly group. His words rang in my ears, 'happy' so out of place in this barbed-wire hell. Willie snuck into my barrack later that night with a present—a fresh slice of bread.

Sunday was our day off at Jawischowitz. That meant cleaning the camp instead of working the mines. Every fourth Sunday Dr Mengele came to visit. In anticipation of his arrival the Kapos would select a group of men either injured, sick or lacking in energy. These men then paraded for the doctor, performing selected physical feats to prove their continued fitness for work. The Sunday after my fourteenth birthday Tatte paraded for the Doctor. I was sent to clean the toilets.

Later, Willie told me what had happened.

'Hop, you weakling. Right foot first,' Mengele had insisted, and my father started hopping, forcing his brittle bones up and down. Decades earlier my father had slipped on icy ground and broken his left ankle. It had healed without medical intervention and Tatte had forgotten all about it, until the order came to swap feet, and Tatte found his ankle giving way underneath him. My father fell, failed the test, and was taken away by truck.

Willie snuck into my barrack later that night. 'He begged the guards to let him say goodbye to us,' Willie told me.

But the guards ignored my father's plea.

Seven

SEPTEMBER 2000

I'm upstairs in my father's study, trying to decipher from his grimace what he wants me to do.

'Your eyes? Your nose?'

I'm not sure which he wants me to wipe. Usually I'm good at this guessing game. My father will cock an eyebrow and I'll know to wipe the sleep from his eyes. Or he'll start to trace the letter 'L' on his trouser leg and I'll reach for his LightWriter.

This is a new request, and it takes me some time to decipher that pitching his head forward and to the left means 'take me to the toilet'. I count to five out loud and then heave Dad out of his chair, guiding his shuffling feet towards the bathroom, arm in arm, keeping him upright. Each day the trip becomes a little riskier, the likelihood of his falling more real. I get him to the toilet safely, position him at the bowl, unzip him and tactfully turn away until I can no longer hear his flow … my cue to flush the toilet and tuck my father in.

I scan Dad's face but see no trace of self-pity. Or anger. He says it brings us closer. That he's learnt to accept help, even enjoy it. His pride may be a little dented, but it's far from destroyed.

'The secret,' he tells me, 'is to change how you see yourself.'

My father may not be able to wipe himself, but he has learnt to accept help graciously. He has learnt patience and the art of listening, and replaced hours at the office and board memberships with the love of friends and family. By exerting a positive attitude and exercising willpower, he has redefined what makes him strong.

'Illness has changed me—for the better. That's how I can let strangers undress and shower me without hating them for it. I still like myself. Maybe more than ever.'

My father may be okay with having others blow his nose, but I'm not. I don't want to see him helpless, robbed of his freedom, like he saw his father robbed.

We have shared a similar hell, Dad and I, watching our fathers wait for death. My father's Tatte, kept apart from his family by a length of barbed wire and a semi-automatic hand-gun; my father, separated from his children by pain and fatigue and the loss of his speech. Tatte refused food; my Dad, unable to eat it. Both of us condemned to watch our fathers grow thin and silent.

History repeats itself. At least I get to say goodbye.

I sit in my car with the engine idling. I usually avoid shopping centres; they are exhausting and, more often than not, I forget where I've parked my car. I've come today looking for inspiration. It's my father's seventieth birthday and I have no idea what to buy him. I can't give him what he needs; I'm just looking to make him smile.

What he *needs* is that his friends visit, as often as they can. And that when they are with him, they ask how he is feeling. Asking doesn't remind him he has a disease—he knows he is sick. He needs people to stop treating him as though he is altered. He is no different now that he is sick, no less of a man. He can hear them and understand what it is they are trying to say, without the slowed-down speech, without being shouted at. His brain still works, his hearing is good. It's harder for him to enunciate now that the muscles in his tongue are weak, so he needs people to be patient. When friends ask his opinion, he needs them to wait for his answer. He wants his opinion to count.

He doesn't need to hear who else is sick. That other people are suffering doesn't make him feel better. He doesn't want to commiserate. He wants to hear good news. He *wants* to be happy.

I leave the bright lights and overpriced stores, knowing no store-bought gift will make my father smile. I head for his house and silently steal upstairs to his dressing room. I locate a stepladder and, balancing on the top rung, open the cupboard reserved for old albums and family memorabilia. I reach in, fingers outstretched, and, feeling past crocheted tablecloths and honeymoon holiday snaps, find a box I haven't touched in years.

I take it home and open it, relieved to find dozens of Super-8 films, still in their packaging. My mother's labels help me put much of the footage in chronological order, but many spools have no markings. I open the telephone directory, locate an editing company and spend the next two weeks watching black-and-white film of my brothers' first steps, the construction of our first home, and my fairy-themed, third birthday party. For a small fortune the video company splices the highlights together and transfers our lives to VHS videotape. I present the video collage to my father on his seventieth birthday. Peter, Gary, Shaun, Amanda, Lesley and I watch the footage with our children, warmed by the memories, watching our children watch us being children.

I look across at my father. He is smiling, a lopsided half-smile.

I saw my father hold a pen for the last time yesterday. He tried to sign his name but the pen slipped from his fingers, time and again, so he gave up trying. Now I sign documents for him. I ask him if not being able to write makes him sad. He says it's an inconvenience, but no, it doesn't make him sad.

'Last month I could feed myself soup with a spoon. My hands shook and often I spilt more than I swallowed, leaving me angry, cursing my useless fingers, hating mealtimes. Now I can't lift the spoon so Mum feeds me, but I've learnt my lesson. Next month I may not be able to swallow so I accept each spoonful gratefully, lingering over the taste, enjoying each mouthful.'

September 2000

My father motions for me to pull my chair closer. I lean forward. We are so close our knees are touching.

'Celebrate *today*,' my father whispers.

Eight

TUESDAY: CAVALCADE OF SKELETONS

Willie had a way about him, a warmth and charm, that made people want to help him. Even his Kapo, who normally would have shot a prisoner for asking questions, succumbed to Willie's charms.

'They've taken your father to a sanatorium to recuperate,' the Kapo had answered in response to Willie's questioning.

'I don't believe him,' Willie confided later that night. 'Think about it, Emil. Why would Mengele spare Tatte?'

My tears cut across his protestations. 'Tatte—dead? Are you telling me they've killed him, Willie?' I started to cry.

Willie put a hand over my mouth. 'Shh, Emil. Your crying will have us both killed. I didn't say father was dead; only that he's not at a sanatorium. He could be here in the hospital, or at another camp. We'll see him again. Hush now.' Willie hugged me tight and told me what I wanted to hear until, perhaps, we both believed it.

November 1944 brought even colder nights and longer

work weeks. Sunday was now set aside for ditch-digging. At the end of each week we marched five kilometres to Buna-Monowitz, a neighbouring concentration camp, to toil alongside its prisoners, hacking at the frozen countryside. To distract themselves from the frostbite stabbing at their toes, the Buna-Monowitz Jews talked. Their conversations went unchecked, since the guards' earmuffs and scarves dulled their hearing. I was surprised to learn that there were other camps close to ours: dozens of camps spread throughout Poland and Germany, camps set up for the purpose of mass execution. I now understood where Joseph, Vasil, Isaac and Andor had gone.

Weeks passed, and soon we were digging ditches every night by floodlight. Our workload had doubled and our food rations halved. As the days grew icier and the prisoners meaner, boys began to fight over blankets, food and the guards' favours. I now stashed saved morsels in my pockets, rather than under my bunk, and slept as Willie instructed, with my plate and spoon under my head. My roommates left me alone. Willie wasn't as fortunate. Some of his roommates had smuggled knives into his barrack and used them to extort food. Willie was brave but he wasn't stupid; he handed over his dinner. Not everyone did. Willie's friend Erno was found lying in a pool of blood after refusing to part with his soup.

Word spread of a Russian advance. Though no one knew the source of this news, most prisoners hungrily accepted each morsel of hope. 'Why else the rush to build trenches?'

I was not hopeful. The Nazis were too consumed with war to allow defeat. In those harsh, hopeless days, so close to defeat myself, I could have easily slipped into death.

I stayed alive because I knew I was supposed to. I was meant to survive. I'd been directed to join the men's group selected for survival; a Polish woman had fed me; and now our Kapo had taken pity on me.

I had wondered why our Kapo never hit me. He was a sadistic Pole who had, at one time or another, beaten nearly every boy in our barrack.

'You look so much like my son,' he said to me one night, out of earshot of the other boys. 'When I look at you I see little Janek standing before me.'

I'd never thought of our Kapo as someone's father. I couldn't imagine him warming a little boy's hands in his pockets. I couldn't imagine a man beating his own son to death either, and that made me feel a little safer.

Though I tried to focus on living, death continued to confront me. I was forced to watch at least a dozen hangings in Jawischowitz, a standard punishment administered by the Nazis for offences such as stealing, talking or loitering. I hated watching the last gasps for air, the vomit before dying, the hanged man's tongue protruding from his swollen mouth, but I feared the alternative—a severe beating—more.

Then there were the suicides. The guards called them 'attempted escapes', but everyone knew the fences surrounding the camps were electrified. Those who died by electrocution meant to die. They weren't trying to get out. They wanted to die now, not in a week or a month, and not at the hands of an angry Kapo or looking down the barrel of an SS gun.

Tuesday: Cavalcade of Skeletons

Every few days the guards would drag us to the fence perimeter, just in case we hadn't noticed Franko hanging from the wires or seen Juno's body charred by the current. I never dreamt of overpowering officers or scaling walls. When I did dream, I dreamt of Mamme's soft-boiled eggs and cookies, of Sabbath wine and warm *challah*. More often, I had nightmares. It was hard to fall asleep at night when I knew closing my eyes meant letting in the Alsatians. In my nightmares, if I tried to run, the dogs chased me. If I backed away slowly, they came at me slowly. I wanted the nightmares to stop, the real and the imagined. My way wasn't the wire, though. My way was to outlast my captors.

By January 1945, we were on the move again. We weren't given advance notice of a trip, or told why we had to leave. All we knew was that we were walking to a railway station, where we would await transfer to a new work-camp. Flanked by hundreds of armed guards, we abandoned Jawischowitz for the ink-black forest, undernourished, under-dressed and ill prepared for a wintry hike. I spotted Willie up ahead and ran to join him.

We marched for hours in ankle-deep snow, a cavalcade of skeletons, joined by inmates from the surrounding camps of Auschwitz, Birkenau and Buna-Monowitz. Worse than the cold was not knowing where we were going; not knowing if our trek would last an hour, a day or a week. I knew I couldn't last a week. By mid-afternoon we were ordered to change direction. Gunfire erupted in the distance and a rumour slipped through the line of men: Gleiwitz station, where we had been heading, was now under Russian control.

We were ordered off the road and led through a snow-covered field. Willie and I hid ourselves in the centre of the group. To lead was foolish: the deep snowdrifts caused those up ahead to fall, whereas we had the benefit of thousands of footprints within which to steady ourselves. The bodies of those who had faltered or collapsed before us (and been shot) now lined our path with blood. I stepped over or around them, focused only on avoiding being tripped up.

The sun gave way to a night sky awash with orange mortar fire. It must have been midnight before we were given the order to stop walking. We had come to three stables, two already filled with prisoners. Hundreds had crammed into the third and I was moments from claiming my own patch of shelter when a guard, barely visible beneath his woolly cap and scarf, stepped forward and barred my way.

'That's enough of you in there. The rest of you, lie down where you are.'

The guard emphasised his instructions by striking the Jew nearest him across the skull with his rifle butt, sending the prisoner reeling into the snow. I lay down flat, the wet snow soaking through my already sweat-stained cotton uniform. I cursed my pathetic body. If I'd just been able to walk a little faster I would have had shelter for the night. Willie lay down beside me and forced a handful of fresh snow into my mouth. Dinner. I sucked at the snowball and began to cry. Willie started digging. Once he'd fashioned a pit for himself he began to scoop out a hole for me. I slid into it on my belly, as Willie instructed.

Tuesday: Cavalcade of Skeletons

'It will keep out the wind,' he whispered.

It was still half-dark when I woke the next morning. Prisoners were flooding out of the third stable, climbing over each other, frantic to get outside. An old man collapsed beside me, crying. His son had been sleeping beside him when the loft above them, overloaded with prisoners, came crashing down. He had escaped with a shattered right knee, but his son had been killed. And here I was, again, alive. I waited for Willie to open his eyes, then I hugged him.

We resumed our march at daybreak, soon coming to an elevated road, which made walking easier. The guards had grown irritable and now shot at prisoners randomly—in the head, at close range—ordering the closest prisoners to drag the bodies into the irrigation ditches that lined the road.

By midday, starving, exhausted and numb with cold, I'd lost the desire to fight. I couldn't see the point of lasting another mile, just to endure ten more. Death would at least bring me sleep. I looked at the dead below me in the ditches and envied them. I stumbled, but Willie caught me.

'Willie, I can't do this anymore. I've tried. I have. Please leave me. I'm only endangering your life.' Willie looked at me and then walked away, returning moments later with a fellow he introduced as Jacob. Willie stood on my left and told Jacob to stand on my right. Each grabbed me under one arm and, lifting me off the ground, dragged me forward.

'Sleep, little brother,' Willie whispered.

When I woke two days later I was in an open cattle train. Eighty thousand prisoners started the march with us; ten thousand survived. Willie was the reason I survived.

'He's awake!' I heard Willie's voice beside me.

'Here, take some snow, Emil. Eat it. You need strength.'

I opened my mouth and accepted the ice my brother had scraped from the carriage floor. I wanted to thank him, to at least look at him, but my head felt so heavy. I closed my eyes and fell back into a dazed sleep, returning to the nightmare I had been unable to shake since my first night on the march.

I dreamt of a mountain, and in my dream climbed to its peak. I had imagined while labouring up the rock face that my trek would end at a pinnacle overlooking a green valley, split in two by a stream. But when I reached the top, a devil lay in wait. He was clad in a black leather bodysuit and knee-high boots, and his bushy, black tail curled upwards. Pitchfork in hand, the half-man, half-beast lunged at me. I tried to turn back to camp, to run, but the devil was a good aim and the prongs of his fork sank deep. He smiled a broken yellow-toothed smile, and licked the blood that fell from the fork onto his talons. He lifted me into the air so that I could see beyond the mountain, see that there was no valley. Not freedom nor food, just a bubbling, burning inferno.

And then he tossed me into the air, and I fell, down, down towards hell, waking only seconds before hitting the burning liquid.

I replayed this horror movie hourly as I slipped between insensibility and consciousness, saved from dehydration and hypothermia by my brother, no more than a skeleton himself. Three days later we stepped off our carriage and were led through the gates of another concentration camp;

Tuesday: Cavalcade of Skeletons

Willie and I, and perhaps thirty others. The other hundred or so men who had shared our carriage were carted away in wheelbarrows.

I was now a veteran of the concentration-camp circuit. I was so used to dogs and guns, starvation and death that when I walked through the gates of 'Buchenwald' deep in the German forest, my surroundings barely registered. The watchtower may have been more imposing than that of Auschwitz, the electrified fences a little higher, the guards more numerous, the inmates more ghostly, but to me it was just another hell I'd have to survive.

A Kapo met us at the main gate and led us to a small barrack. Inside, seated behind a large wooden desk, was a squat, bald man. On the table before him lay bundles of striped uniforms. A guard stood on each side of the desk. One held a rifle, the other a clipboard.

I undressed and gave my number as instructed.

'Juden,' the guard with the paperwork announced. At this, the bald German rifled through the piles of cloth and produced a jacket with a yellow Star of David upon it and a pair of pants. I slipped them on, noticing a new number in black print etched beside the star on the jacket. My new name.

I followed the column of men emerging from the barrack into Buchenwald's main square for evening roll-call. Willie was pinching his cheeks and they began to glow pink amidst the sea of white, wan faces.

'It's Jacob's trick. Makes you look healthy enough to work,' Willie whispered, pointing to the sign looming overhead: *Arbeit Macht Frei*—'work sets you free'. I pinched my cheeks and stood to attention next to Willie, scanning the lines of men to my left and right, searching for familiar faces from Jawischowitz. Bald, pale and feeble, their eyes dull, their faces gaunt, the men around me looked no more alive than the dead who had been carried off the carriages moments before.

I looked at Willie. He looked no better.

Most of the prisoners were Jews. The remainder had either red, green or black triangles on their uniforms.

'Red are political prisoners. Green are criminals. Keep away from the black, they're murderers,' Willie whispered.

Thankfully, the yellow stars were herded together. We were placed in the *Alte Lager* (old camp), a huge barrack—number 66. At least three hundred others shared our living quarters. I was squeezed between Willie and a silent, sad man, whose name I never learnt, on the third tier of a four-storey bunk bed. An identical expanse of wooden boards lay across from us, separated by a wide passage. Men lay spooned together on the splintering wood without mattresses or blankets. To turn from left to right I had to climb down from the bunk and pull myself up again.

We didn't have to work in Buchenwald. Besides the usual cleaning duties and roll-call, our days were unoccupied. Confined to our barracks, we were left to lapse into depression, observe the onset of disease, and obsess over the lack of food. No longer busy with work, I longed for company and the consolation of conversation. Talking was forbidden at Buchenwald. Initially I risked a whispered word, a muffled remark, a hushed discussion. We usually talked about food or freedom; rarely death. Then one day I was caught on the rim of a group, on the outskirts of a discussion. The Kapo's stick snapped at my back and I heard the crack of bone. Willie, who was nearby, pulled me from the sweep of the stick, and led me back to the barrack. I rarely talked after that and I never walked on the edge of a crowd again. I hid in the middle.

One Friday our boredom was relieved by an outing. We were taken to the main camp to join other prisoners at an exhibition of lampshades, gloves and handbags. I thought it strange that we prisoners were considered worthy of such an event, but still I enjoyed the distraction of the display.

Then a Kapo explained the outing. 'A fine example of German craftsmanship and ingenuity,' he said. 'Who would have thought Jewish skin could be turned into such fine, pliable leather!'

I filed out of the hall, nauseated and feeling defeated. We weren't just losing our lives; the world was losing its humanity. My beliefs battered, I contemplated suicide. I made elaborate plans to end my life: I would jump from a truck on the way to work, the guards would see me and shoot, and it would all be over. Or, I'd wander from my barrack to the watchtower and the guards would yell 'get back' but I'd just keep walking.

I imagined doing these things, but when the time came, I couldn't do them.

Within a few weeks I developed a growth on the back of my neck. It soon grew to the size of a tennis ball, and Willie insisted I show it to the camp orderly. He, in turn, admitted me to the hospital where I was led to a white-tiled room and told to undress. Naked, I climbed onto a hardwood table, shivering as I saw four lengths of rope laid out on the floor. A nurse picked the strands off the floor, indicating by pressing a bony finger to my back that I was to lie face down on the table. I stretched out and waited, the wood cold against my cheek, as the nurse silently wound a length of rope around each of my limbs, fixing me to the operating table. As she pulled the last knot taut, an elderly man entered the room clutching a kitchen knife, the type Mamme used for slicing beef. Without stopping to wash the dirt from his fingernails or administer an anaesthetic, the doctor made an incision on my neck. I felt nails tearing at flesh and a great pressure, and then I saw blood on the floor. And then it was over, the worst pain I'd ever experienced, and he was wiping the pus on his hands onto his apron.

The nurse untied me, bandaged my neck and led me to a bed, the first bed I had slept in since I'd left home. Five other patients shared my six-bed ward, which was overseen by two tired, but kindly, male nurses. I spent three days in hospital, mostly in bed, reluctant to leave the comfort of my mattress and warmth of my blankets. An old Polish Jew lay next to me, his right eye bandaged.

'The butchers—they took it right out. Just because it was crusty. Hardly examined it first.'

The old Pole liked to talk and, starved for conversation, I happily engaged him. I had grown proficient in Polish under the conveyor belt, thanks to Zosia, so I listened intently and learnt from the Pole the secrets of Buchenwald.

'Did you hear of the Slovak boy, taken by the doctors and pumped with medicines to make him grow? He died last night.'

And the next day: 'They dragged a young man in

yesterday and cut off his testicles. I heard his nurses talking. Groundbreaking research, they called it.'

The old Pole tried to answer all my questions.

'Why operate on us? Why not let us die like the rest?' I asked from my bed.

The old Pole guessed that the hospital existed to satisfy the Red Cross, to comply with war-time convention.

He couldn't answer my other question, the one that kept me from sleep. None of us knew why God was hiding from the Nazis, letting them kill us, the innocent and the young. Letting them win.

Willie snuck in to see me every day. I shared with him what I had learnt, though he hardly seemed surprised by my stories. Did he know about the medical experiments at Buchenwald? Had he seen the crematoria?

'I'm meant to be released tomorrow,' I told Willie, 'but I think I'll stay a while.'

The next morning when the doctor came to visit, I tried Joseph's trick. Hiding the thermometer under my blanket, I rubbed it vigorously, massaging the temperature up three degrees. I stayed in hospital another four days. When, on my eighth day, I handed in my real temperature, I was discharged immediately. I said goodbye to my friend the Pole, and told him I was being released to barrack four, the Russian youth barrack; my old barrack was full. The Pole pulled me towards him and tore the Star of David from my jacket arm, whispering, 'Don't tell them you're a Jew. They'll eat you for dinner.'

The Russian barrack—a mix of Russian civilians and German communist sympathisers—was like heaven, after barrack 66, despite the stress of living a deception. Having learnt Yiddish, I could communicate with the German boys, and told them I was the son of a communist, imprisoned for anti-German behaviour. I hid myself in the showers to avoid revealing my religion, and the lie worked: the boys treated me as one of their own.

Sometimes Willie snuck in to visit. He called my barracks 'the palace' on account of the living room, mattresses, blankets, pillows, cold-water tap and indoor toilet. Each of the five bedrooms contained only two sets of bunks. We spent most of our time in the kitchen so I could sneak Willie food without the other boys noticing. Willie ate the same basic food in his barrack, but our bread ration was doubled and the ingredients delivered raw. The washed, peeled and boiled produce, free of disease, and cooked up by our own boys, tasted so much better. Sometimes I'd sneak Willie bread. It was as stale as his handout, but came topped with jam, butter and, occasionally, sausage.

'A little extra for Jacob,' I'd whisper, pressing a slice of cabana into his palm.

The Russians believed that the war would end soon. Their enthusiasm was infectious, and soon I, too, dared to think of a future. I kept death and gloom outside by staying in the barrack whenever I could. Eventually, danger found its way in. I'd come back from showering, wrapped in the thinnest of towels. It had been raining so the barrack was full. Boys lay on their bunks, restless and bored. I was conscious that Josef, who lay on the bunk nearest mine, should not see my towel slip, so I gripped it tightly as I tried to slip into my pants. The German smiled at me, his curiosity piqued.

'What's the story, Emil? Do you think we fancy you?

You're holding that towel so tight your knuckles are turning white.'

Heinrich, two beds down, piped up. 'I've got it! It's because he's so small. Yeah, that's it. He's embarrassed of his microscopic dick.'

Pretty soon I was surrounded. Boys were taking bets, guessing measurements, and I was sweating. I didn't want to think what they'd do to me if they pulled the towel from me, and discovered I was circumcised. A Jew and a liar!

I was backed into a corner, fingers reaching towards me. Big smiles. Wide eyes. Ludwig, the oldest boy, pushed through the group, stopping only inches from my towel. The barrack grew quiet. I closed my eyes and waited for the unveiling. Ludwig came no closer. Instead, turning his back to me, he addressed the group, 'Show's over, men. Leave the little boy alone; we were all small once.' Throwing my pants at me, Ludwig winked.

April arrived. The air grew less chilly, and snow gave way to mud. Rumours circled of an American approach. I knew that Berlin had ordered the immediate liquidation of all camps because each day another barrack was emptied.

Willie came to visit. 'I'm leaving tomorrow, Emil. Ten thousand of us are being transported to some factory to work. Apparently your barrack—the young Russians—are being left till last, with the cooks and cleaners. We won't be apart for long.'

And then he was gone.

Although we'd spent most of our time in separate barracks, somehow I still felt Willie was essential to my wartime existence. Seeing his face at roll-call each morning got me through the day. Without his silent support, I didn't know how to make it through. So I didn't try; I spent the day in bed. At sunset I found out I was to be reunited with Willie sooner than I'd thought — my barrack's transportation was slated for the next day.

I woke early on Wednesday, 11 April 1945, eager for the move. As the sun rose with no sign of our Kapo, boys tentatively began to inch towards the windows. I followed, and saw through the bars sentry guards fleeing their posts. Ludwig opened the door and crept outside. I followed him to the main square. Incredibly, it was deserted.

Word spread fast that the last of the guards had fled into the forest, carrying civilian garb filched from the prisoners, shedding their uniforms as they ran. The US Army was poised to strike. Within minutes, the square was teeming with prisoners — now free men, but too scared to celebrate the shock desertion. I continued to follow Ludwig around the camp, hiding among the boys who had joined his search, still protecting myself from attack. Ludwig found a ladder and climbed into the office of the camp commandant. When the telephone rang, Ludwig picked up the receiver and answered in German. Finally he descended the ladder, his face drawn.

'That was Berlin,' Ludwig announced to the crowd that had gathered around him. 'A convoy of Hitler Youth is on its way to Buchenwald.' Being German, Ludwig had easily passed himself off as the camp commandant.

'They have instructions to kill us,' he continued. 'But

we won't let them! The end of the war is too close. Arm yourselves. Search for rifles, sticks, stones, anything.'

So, this will be my end, I thought, bending to scoop up a stone. Murdered by Hitler's children during the last gasps of war. I shot up at the roar of airplanes screaming overhead. Packages were falling from the sky like hailstones. A brown box thudded at my feet, the word 'Aid' scrawled along its top.

'Look!' the boy next to me yelled, pointing at a huge American tank approaching from the right.

'Over there,' another boy shouted, pointing to the column of Hitler Youth marching towards us from the left. I stood, immobile, as the two groups clashed metres from me, watching a war rage, as if it were a performance in which I played no part. My future was being determined outside Buchenwald's main gate. If the wrong side lost, I was dead.

Nine

MARCH 2000

'What's dying like?' I ask my father. I'm seated on the edge of his bed, the hospital curtains drawn around us. Only visitors close the curtains; the patients in shared rooms have already laid everything bare: sponge baths, bed pans, catheters.

I wait for him to stop scribbling and turn the block of paper towards me.

'Peaceful.'

Two days ago, laid flat on an emergency-department trolley in a back cubicle, feverish and drowsy with pneumonia, my father had begun to slip away. His neck brace, usually removed for sleep, was pressing on his windpipe, robbing him of air. Too weak to speak, my father could not tell the nurse on duty that he was choking.

'The visual send-off was breathtaking,' he continues to write. 'I saw Porubka and then the death camps. One scene melted into the next. I was on a train to Bonegilla, the dusty red earth swirling around me and then there was your mother, just as she was the first time I met her, dark hair and smiling eyes. She took my hand and her belly swelled with you and we were at Mount Buller building snowmen with your brothers, waiting for your arrival. And then, there you were, in white, at your wedding. Everything softened at the edges, bathed in sunshine.'

Dad is sweating now and tired.

'I knew I was dying,' he continues to write, his scrawl almost illegible. 'I could hear myself struggling to breathe, but I wasn't scared. I'd had a good life, I was ready. But then I opened my eyes and you were all there and a great warmth passed through me. I looked at you all loving me, wanting me to stay, and I knew I wanted to go on living.'

Noticing on the monitors a sudden drop in my father's oxygen level, my mother had run from his cubicle, screaming for assistance. By then, my father was blue. A nurse came, and then another, and then the doctors came running, and a code blue was called. My father was taken to the resuscitation area, his shirt cut away, his face covered with an oxygen mask and, finally, his collar pulled from his neck.

Death extended its hand again, twelve hours later, when a twenty-centimetre plastic pipe was forced down his nose. My father knew frequent suctioning was necessary to draw the phlegm from his lungs. Each time the tube scraped his throat it was so painful he thought of giving up, but then it was over and he opened his eyes and saw my mother.

'I must have died a hundred deaths those first three days in intensive care,' he writes.

I take the pen from his hand and the pad from his lap,

and cupping his head with my left hand, I remove one of his cushions and lay his head down, flat.

❦

It's only been four days, but I miss Dad's voice already. We stole it from him. It was the easiest thing we ever did.

'You have a choice,' Dr Irving had said. But we didn't really. If my father didn't have a tracheostomy, he would die; the sputum would drown him. If we kept suctioning it away the pain would kill him. So we let the doctors take his voice, to give him life.

I hadn't known that he'd been favouring death to spare us the worst of the disease. I didn't know that he cried the entire hour we were deliberating with the doctor. I didn't know that his mind was already made up, but that seeing us gathered around his bedside, bleary-eyed, had changed his mind. He'd looked at us and, realising his departure would hurt us, reprimanded himself for welcoming the end.

Dr Irving started to speak, but my father cut him off with a whisper, his last words, 'I want to live. I want the tracheostomy.'

❦

My father has a hole in his throat. The doctors thought that by cutting into his body they would extend his life. Instead they gave him a new one. A silent, textureless, odour-free world. He can no longer whisper or sigh out loud, taste his favourite food or smell his wife's perfume. The surgeon's

March 2000

blade severed more than skin.

He dreams of speaking. In these dreams he is with friends. They sit at cafés drinking coffee or dine at each other's homes. He can't recall what they talk about. He just remembers the feeling of putting sound to his thoughts. Of tossing words into the air, trading sentences, offering opinions, being heard. Of arguing for the sake of it and telling a joke.

He wakes with the taste of conversation on his lips, momentarily unaware of his disease. Then the starched white sheets come into focus and he tries to say something and nothing comes out. He buzzes for the nurse, motions to the bed pan. Sometimes she walks right by, knowing he needs her, pretending not to see. Mostly she comes, after a time, and by then he's wet the bed and she has to change him. It can take twenty minutes to explain how to get his pillows just right. He is not a patient man. He's learning.

I don't remember dreams. Sometimes I wake, knowing I've just returned from another place, that my baby daughter's midnight cries have torn me from a tale, but I can't go back. Except in this one dream.

I'm at a dinner party. The setting is unimportant, the guests irrelevant. My father sits slumped in his wheelchair beside my mother, his chin resting heavily on his padded neck brace, the tracheostomy filter poking from his neck. Our company, oblivious to my father's condition, talk freely of world affairs, the state of the economy, the latest place to dine.

'So what do you think, Emil?' one of the group asks.

I lean forward to fill the silence, to explain it, when my father responds. My mother has taken off his collar and detached his filter and he's speaking.

A part of me still believes that if I ripped that tube out, if my father tried really hard, his voice—the voice I hear only when I call his house and get the answering machine—would come back. Part of me still believes the disease *is* the dream.

❦

They've ordered beer and coffee. They sit in wheelchairs, in slippered feet, faces turned towards the sun, or lie propped up on pillows, beds doubling as sun-lounges. Portable suction machines, syringes and rubber gloves are packed into trolleys, the splintered outdoor setting disguised under a yellow plastic tablecloth. A vase from Bed Twenty adorns the table, a spray of synthetic colour fans from the glass. The ward has been emptied of sickness and the patio transformed for Friday's happy hour. The patients—some still discovering, some dealing with disease, all dying—celebrate the sunshine.

I step onto the verandah and smile. A nurse takes my order: hot chocolate, two sugars. Ron, lying in his bed at the far end of Café Hospitale takes his coffee black, through a tube. A nurse massages sun cream into exposed legs and drops sunhats onto heads. Brian is feeling tipsy; it's been a long time since he's downed a beer. He misses the taste, he tells us, but he'll take it any way he can.

'My shout,' laughs Dad's nurse. 'What'll it be?'

My father shakes his head, then extends his left finger in the direction of the double doors, as if to say 'give mine to her'. Joan lies just inside the swinging doors, within earshot of the festivities, her body encased in an iron cocoon, a giant lung.

My father doesn't want to get drunk. He's already lost control: of his limbs, his speech, his life.

I skirt the group, scrape a plastic chair towards my father and take his hand. He blinks at me, the same exaggerated blink he offered up throughout my childhood and adolescence, a blink that meant 'I love you and I'm proud of you', when distance or propriety dictated he not say the words out loud. I'd seen that blink so many times before—looking down at him from school-concert stages, from behind a piano, from the upper balcony at synagogue. A blink that now would have to say so much more.

His legs glow white beneath the pale-blue hospital gown. It's been a week since the tracheostomy tube took his voice. I pull a clipboard and pen from my bag and slide it under my father's right hand. He looks from me to his hands—up and down, up and down. Eventually I understand and pull the lid off the pen.

'I'm going home,' he writes. 'I'll make it out of here.' He looks sick, a dangerous yellow. I don't know if he'll walk again, if his lungs will overcome the pneumonia. They won't tell me how long he's got. I repeat his words out loud, giving shape to his thoughts. I believe him.

Ten

WEDNESDAY: THE TASTE OF CHOCOLATE

After a time, the spray of machine-gun fire thinned, then stopped.

Tanks, armoured scout cars and motorised artillery circled the camp, finally passing through Buchenwald's main gate before sunset. Two American officers had words with a group of Russian and German inmates and we fell into line again. This time we waited for biscuits, soap and chocolate. We waited quietly. I didn't cheer or dance or rush to hug our American liberators. Those who did hung on to the army personnel more out of desperation and disbelief than joy. A strange sorrow pervaded the camp. Prisoners devoured food torn from aid packages, trying to make up for all the missed meals, surprised to find that when sated, their emptiness persisted. Celebrating felt wrong; too many had died.

I had questions, but how to acquaint my stomach with food was not one of them. I tore open a food parcel and began to unfurl a chocolate bar from its wrapper.

Wednesday: The Taste of Chocolate

'This is what I'll do with the rest of my life,' I told myself, 'eat chocolate.'

I closed my eyes, blocking out everything—my shaking knees, itchy scalp, twisting bowels—focusing instead on the square of cocoa melting on my tongue. I unwrapped a second bar, meditating on the creamy dark sweetness, and then a third.

'Take it easy, Emil,' an inmate from my barrack cautioned. 'Start on bread and crackers. Stick to bland foods for now. Give your stomach time to adjust.'

Out of habit, I followed orders. I stuck to a safe diet and, helped by the fact that I had been in the youth barrack, I adjusted well. It was hard tempering my hunger when those around me gorged themselves on meat, cheese and cream biscuits. Harder still to watch these same men days later, writhing in pain as their stomachs contorted, soiling themselves before they reached the toilet stalls, and, once there, unable to drag themselves from the pits. Death continued to stalk the camp; hundreds died of diarrhoea. Typhoid and cholera swept through the barracks. For many, freedom came too late.

What I needed even more desperately than food was information about Willie. I wanted to step beyond the barbed wire and into our new lives together. I discovered his whereabouts from Jacob, his best friend, who returned to camp the following day.

'Jacob, where's Willie? Why isn't he with you?'

My words were silenced by a hug. A hug that was a little too desperate, a little too long.

I pulled back; Jacob was crying.

'Please, Jacob, I need to know,' I persisted.

His report was punctuated with tears.

Willie and Jacob had been on the last transport out of Buchenwald the day before liberation. They had been taken by truck to a forest and assembled around a pit. Jacob was positioned, teetering at the edge. Willie was three or four rows back, in the outermost circle. Jacob had peered in and seen bodies at the bottom of the pit. He'd been glad his friend hadn't seen them. Then the shooting began. Jacob didn't see Willie fall, but my brother was on the outer rim, closer to the guns, so Jacob concluded they must've gotten him first. Jacob blacked out. Next thing he remembered, he was awake, in the pit. He wasn't bleeding or hurt, so he figured he must have fallen in or collapsed under the force of all the bodies behind him. He remembered it was hard getting out, getting past the flesh pressing down on him and the blood—blood everywhere. But he struggled to the top and lay still, on top of the heap, until nightfall, when, together with seven other survivors, he crawled from the pit to hide in a nearby forest and wait. Willie never came.

My brother Willie, funny and brave. He saved my life more than once, risking his own to feed and carry me through the war. Willie had worked so much harder than me to survive. He was stronger than me, more hopeful and resourceful. Of the two of us, he was the one more deserving of life.

I cried myself to sleep every night for three weeks. I cried for Willie, for myself, for the loss of my family. If Willie was dead, I reasoned, strong, smart Willie, then the rest were surely dead, too.

I needed to find someone deserving of life who *had* made

Wednesday: The Taste of Chocolate

it, so I went in search of my friend, the old Pole. I wanted to thank him for his invaluable advice. I found out he was back in the hospital, this time with typhoid. I raced to his ward but was stopped at the door by a nurse.

'You're too late,' she said. 'He died this morning.'

Death followed me around the camp. I was free to roam the grounds, to open doors and inspect buildings, but instead of feeling free, I felt oppressed. I saw for the first, frightening time the rumoured crematoria. I saw bodies stacked and waiting to be burnt, and rooms cleared of all furniture, their floors littered with objects of torture: vices, clamps, racks. I'd been scared in the camps—sad, depressed, hopeless, sickened—but never angry. Now I felt enraged. I'd always thought of myself, of the Jews, as incidental to the war, as accidental victims. I looked at the human ovens, the timetables, schedules and charts and realised that we were the target. And that realisation changed things. It wasn't any longer just about what they'd done to me; it was what they intended to do to all of us, the Jewish people—our obliteration.

Gangs sprang up and I joined one. Armed with sticks and stones we invaded German villages. We broke windows, stole chickens and threw eggs at German houses. We damaged machinery, broke fences and drove cattle from their paddocks. It was exciting and empowering and the only way I knew how to even the score with these people who had closed their eyes to Hitler and let their sons don his uniforms. I wanted them to taste fear, to be scared, really scared, so I spent my days filling my pockets with stones, and my nights driving German women and children to hide behind locked doors. I didn't feel bad and I didn't feel guilty. I felt entitled, and so I felt unjustly treated when, two weeks later, the American Military Police demanded an end to the violence. We were to show the world we were better than our oppressors.

'And if you don't toe the line,' the military police threatened, 'you'll be placed under house arrest.'

For those of us wishing to return home, it was a powerful threat.

We were transferred to the SS officers' quarters. Their life of luxury, of beds with thick mattresses, pillowcases and blankets, seemed perverse. It took me a long time to sleep well on those clean, white sheets.

'How old are you? Ten? Eleven?' The American relief worker measuring me for clothes refused to believe I was fourteen.

'You sure are tiny,' the girl said, handing me the smallest pair of pants she could find. I put them on and turned up the cuffs four times. My new shoes were three sizes too big and my shirt gaped at the neck. With my fingers hidden under impossibly long sleeves, I looked like a thrift-store clown, but I felt like a million dollars.

I told my story to anyone wanting to hear it, garnering attention from United Nations representatives, various American care organisations and a swag of Jewish aid groups, all intrigued by one so small and young surviving the camps.

They offered me a future, the future I'd dreamt of at my first-grade desk: American citizenship, a house with a family, and a chance to complete my education. I wanted to accept the airline ticket and leave right away. The kindness of the

Wednesday: The Taste of Chocolate

American officers and volunteers, and the quality of their Hershey's chocolate steeled my resolve to make their rich country my own, but I politely declined. I wasn't going to be resettled yet, not until I'd returned to Porubka. Not until I knew whether or not my family had survived.

※

I left the officers' quarters, and my days recuperating in the spring sunshine, with mixed feelings. I was ready to return home but sad to leave. I'd changed in those last weeks, grown more confident. I'd stopped looking over my shoulder, standing to attention when addressed, and hiding in the centre of a group. I wasn't shovelling food into my mouth at a frantic pace, now trusting that there would be another meal tomorrow. I'd put on weight and built muscle, but it was more than that. I believed again. Not in God, but in myself. I finally felt human, after all those months of neglect, insult and abuse, because those around me—the kitchen-hands, aid workers, military personnel, reporters—believed I was human. People called me by my name, they cared whether I was hungry, they wanted to know how I felt. My future was important to them. For the first time in my life, outside of my family, I felt I was an *equal*. It felt good to be with good people.

I headed for home, frightened to learn that the rest of my family were dead, too. A small part of me still dared to hope that Tatte, Mamme, Alex, Rozsi and Cili were alive and waiting for me.

It seemed the whole world was on the move. People were either heading home or heading out, scrambling to start a new life, searching for a new home. The authorities assisted in this task by procuring free transport and meals for camp inmates. The trains leaving Germany were full, but if you were quick, there was still space up top. I scaled a train wall and, ducking to avoid tunnels and bridges, spent the next three weeks on the roof of a train, following the curve of the tracks that would take me home.

Solly, an ex-prisoner, cut short my meditation.

'There's an SS man down below in civilian clothes, trying to go unnoticed. Anyone care to join me? I'm about to conduct an interview,' he announced.

I jumped at the chance, filing into the suspect's carriage after Solly and his mates. We stood silently around the suspect's seat, waiting for the bastard to look up, eight sets of eyes fixed on his dark-blond scalp. The German kept his eyes trained on his newspaper. The printing under his hot, sweaty fingers began to smudge. Solly looked over at his friends and nodded. Three of the group jumped the officer and pinned him down, allowing Solly to get at his gun.

'Strip,' demanded Solly, pressing the weapon to its owner's head, 'or we'll make you.' Solly's voice was surprisingly strong for one so feeble.

The German refused to move.

'I'm a farmer, a German living off the land. I know nothing of the SS or army.'

We didn't believe him. He was tall, strong and healthy.

Wednesday: The Taste of Chocolate

The army would have claimed him. Solly grabbed the man's hands and turned them over, so that his palms were visible. They were smooth. No farmyard calluses. Aided by his friends, Solly ripped off the German's shirt to reveal, below the man's left arm, an SS tattoo.

I went crazy, punching, kicking, scratching. A knee to the stomach for my father, a left hook to his head for my mother, a twisted arm for my sisters. I wanted to hurt him like he'd hurt Willie, the old Pole, Joseph, Andor and all the others. He was the Third Reich and I wanted to kill him.

The train stopped to refuel and Solly pulled me off the German. An inspector entered, asking for tickets—and the officer, stripped to his waist and bleeding, fled the compartment, pursued by Solly and his angry group. When they jumped from the train, I jumped off, too. But by the time I'd caught up with them, the officer was half-dead and the older boys wouldn't let me at him.

'I promise I won't punch him. I just want to see that he's dead,' I begged. I needed an end, something more than a flag or an abandoned watchtower. A guard without a weapon, with his heart stopped, with a prisoner—his prisoner—standing over him: that would be a fitting end to my war.

'Emil, it's over,' Solly whispered, turning my head from the mess. 'Get back on the train. Go home.'

I reboarded the train and scrambled to the roof. Everyone wanted answers.

'What happened to the Nazi? Did you get him?'

They needed to hear that we had, in some small measure, evened the score. I didn't want to talk about it. Instead, I focused on the tracks as they disappeared under the train. It was time to move on, time to look forward.

I found myself thinking about Porubka, about our house and the dusty dirt floors and sleeping next to Rozsi in front of the fire. About making *challah* with Mamme, sharing an apple with Cili in the back room of the general store, sitting with Tatte at Shul, pulling my trousers down for Wasserman's cane, cleaning the school toilets, playing alone.

After zigzagging through Germany, Austria and Hungary, I made it to Ungvar where I found, by asking around at the soup kitchens, synagogues and markets, that my brother Alex was still alive, and living in the nearby country town of Velke Kapusany. It was rumoured that Rozsi and Cili were on their way to join him. No one had heard about my parents.

It was a mild June night, so I slept in a park under a blanket of stars. The next day I boarded a train for Porubka, but it didn't feel like a homecoming. Porubka had always been somewhere I'd wanted to escape from, and when I stepped into the main street after an eighteen-month absence, I felt just as much a stranger as I had ever been. I walked the length of the main street, past children I'd grown up with and men who had bartered with my father. No one smiled and no one stopped me. I headed up the hill towards our house, surprised to see it so unchanged; the flowerbeds my mother had tended were still flowering. The door of the general store was wide open. I quickened my pace.

'Can I help you?' a young woman with metallic grey eyes asked, but it wasn't a question. She stood in front of our store, barring the entrance, this woman, this stranger, clearly not a friend of Mamme's. I turned towards the house and saw the front door swing open and three children with puzzled looks glance at their mother, and then at me, waiting for an explanation. I was the stranger here, the one who didn't belong.

I turned and ran until I ended up at my old school, looking through my first-grade classroom window. It was summer break and Mr Lukac was absent from his desk. I wiped an arc across the dusty window-pane and saw more clearly the blackboard, scrubbed clean. And then I saw myself, aged six, back to the board, arms pinned down and the boys from the front row, taking advantage of the teacher's absence, drawing a Star of David on my forehead with chalk. I walked on, stopping at the school principal's window. It wasn't hard to conjure up Tatte's image, sitting stern and straight in the visitor's chair. Tatte had been a regular visitor to the school, though he certainly was not the principal's favourite. My father would complain of my mistreatment, and week after week the principal would do nothing. Eventually Tatte gave up on the man, choosing instead to lecture my peers. I was so embarrassed. Not because Tatte preached equality and tolerance in the schoolyard, but because he chose his audience so poorly. They didn't even pretend to listen.

I spent the morning reliving mostly miserable memories, sometimes changing the endings. I washed my dusty hands in the icy waters of the neighbouring creek, shivering at the memory of being thrown in. I went to synagogue. I wasn't planning on finding God, just my old seat, maybe stay for a song or two. I needed to know my religion had survived, even if most of its followers hadn't. I didn't make it to my seat. I couldn't get to the front door; there was too much barbed wire. It didn't matter. I wouldn't be spending another Sabbath here.

I sat by the roadside and watched my former neighbours. Did they avert their eyes out of guilt? We would have been easy to hide, my blue-eyed, pale-faced siblings and I. No one offered. No one tried.

'Guilt? We're not guilty.' I imagined them saying.

But I did find them guilty. Guilty of lending their silent support. Guilty of knowing everything, yet doing nothing to stop Hitler. I looked around and saw a town consumed with hatred, a repository for all the evil and ignorance in the world. If I could assign death to the camps, and bury hatred in Porubka, in its people, then I could allow for life and hope and a future somewhere else.

'You can keep the business and our home,' I yelled at no one in particular.

Eleven

FEBRUARY 2002

My father never talked about the war unless we asked, and then it was only to regale us with the stories he thought we could handle: the sanitised version. He told us of marching through the snow but not of the dead by the roadside. He mentioned working at the mines but never talked of dismembered limbs. He spoke of hunger, not starvation, and death instead of murder.

'That's the past,' my father used to say. 'You are my future.'

I knew I had done nothing to reassemble his life. He'd let go of any anger long before I came on the scene. Apart from a nervous tic—a barely discernible tilting of his head in the direction of his right shoulder—you'd never guess my father was one of the wounded. I grew up encouraged to trust in people, to see the good in them, to take risks and love life. Only now do I see how easy it would have been for my father to teach me hatred and suspicion. For him to rail against the unfairness of this second blow.

Only now does his ordinariness seem so extraordinary.

❦

I commit my father's story to paper, straining to craft the perfect sentence. To embroider each page with my father's experience, to infuse the space between words with his spirit. My father just wants to connect sound to his thoughts.

'It hurts that I can't talk to you,' he types. I know that for him this is the hardest part. Not the dead arms or heavy head. Not the pain, the unrelenting exhaustion or missed meals. What torments him most is being shut in. Shut up. Muzzled. Crying out in frustration but sending nothing into the air.

I try it one day: silence. I sit in my chair in my study, hang my arms by my side, make myself heavy in my chair, just like Dad. Looking out at the garden, at the flowers, I kill the instinct to call my son Josh from his playroom to share the eruption of colour. The phone rings and I let the machine take a message, resisting the urge to pick up. I listen. This is how everyday life is for my father: all one-way conversation. I turn to my desk. A pile of bills threatens to spill from my in-tray. I don't reach for the chequebook or straighten the pile. I sit tethered and mute, the silence teasing. I last half an hour.

❦

'The disease has changed him,' I tell my best friend. 'My father is a different person now. He has grown. Deepened.'

My friend smiles. 'I see you're still wearing those rose-coloured glasses.'

'A gift from my father. I've worn them since birth,' I joke, but it's true. The bright side was the only side I got to see. Still get to see.

'I'm a lucky man,' my father tells me.

He sees that I'm incredulous. By definition, if you can't say the words 'I'm lucky', if you have to rely on a computer chip to speak for you, you are not lucky.

Still, he insists. 'How many people get advance warning of their death and the opportunity to tell family and friends they love them? Time to plan those last months and live out postponed dreams? I wake up every day and you know what I do?' my father asks.

I shake my head.

'I walk around this house — the house your mother and I built thirty-four years ago — and fall in love with it all over again. With the house and with my life and with the memories. It's all been a bonus, Suzy, every day since liberation.'

I get to say goodbye. I guess I should be thankful. There's nothing that's been left unsaid or undone. No secrets. No regrets. Dad has let me into his world completely and unashamedly. Shared his life and his struggles with me, letting down his guard in a way fathers rarely do, thinking they have to be strong and driven, instead of what their children really want them to be. Around.

It was only after we'd said goodbye that we really introduced ourselves. The fact that there wasn't a tomorrow allowed us to strip away the excuses and ask the embarrassing and uncomfortable questions. Forced us to clear our calendars and make time for each other. Tell one another that we loved each other, for no reason except that next year maybe we couldn't. So, yes, I should be thankful.

But I'm not. I'm not nearly ready for him to leave. I've only just started listening, now that he's stopped talking. Funny how you listen so much harder when someone is whispering. As a child I never had to strain to hear what my father was saying. With the volume always turned up, the neighbours didn't have to strain. Dad had a big voice. His opinions were never subtle, and he never whispered. When Dad entered a room he filled it. When he joined a conversation, he took over. Dad ran a business, his family, the local council and our Jewish community. He was everywhere.

Part of me admired his bravado, but mostly I was embarrassed by it. As a teenager all I wanted to do was fit in. Dad only knew how to stand out. So, rather than encourage him, I ignored him. The louder he was, the less I listened.

He hasn't changed. He still doesn't give a damn what people think of him. The thing is, I'm no longer embarrassed. I look at him receiving guests in his study, sitting with his fly half-open, a rubber band looped around the tag of his zip, and I'm proud of him. He doesn't ask his guests to leave the room, nor does he apologise when Mum removes his collar and filter to feed a forty-centimetre catheter into his tracheostomy tube. He just asks that his guests speak a little louder, so that he might hear them over the buzz of the electric suctioning device. His guests are invited to wipe the sweat from his forehead and help him from his chair.

He's not consciously setting out to teach them. But by

refusing to allow the feeding and suctioning and outward signs of decay to divert their attention, by making them sit and wait for the LightWriter to verbalise his thoughts, he's giving them, giving us all, a lesson in compassion.

Twelve

THURSDAY: ESCAPE

I headed north-east to Velke Kapusany to find my brother and sisters. Alex opened the door and saw me first, his screams drawing his sisters to the front of the house. Rozsi froze at the doorway, her mouth the only part of her capable of moving, 'Emil' the only word her lips could shape. She watched her younger sister grab me hard and propel me backwards, to get a better look at their little brother, still alive, so alive.

'His hair is thick and curly,' Cili said, turning to Rozsi.

'He's alive,' whispered Rozsi, and we all held hands. I looked at my siblings. They looked tired. In those first days of family, we talked little of war, preferring the warmth of each others' bodies to words. When we spoke, it was in turns, to exchange stories.

'Willie is dead,' I told Alex, Rozsi and Cili. 'Tatte, too. Mengele took him.'

Alex bowed his head. 'And Mamme makes three.'

Thursday: Escape

Rozsi ran from the room and Alex followed her.

'What happened to Mamme, Cili?' I shifted closer to my sister and took her trembling hand.

Cili wouldn't look at me but she began to talk.

'She was taken from us in Birkenau,' Cili whispered. 'After you men left, they divided us up again. She was sent off with the sick and the elderly. She was only forty-six. Not like the rest. She was strong. You remember, Emil. She could cart a whole pot of stew to the oven, without help. "Strong as an ox," Tatte would say, "and just as hardworking." She shouldn't have gone to the left. She should've stayed with us.'

'Where did she go, Cili?' I needed to hear the words from my sister.

'To the crematoria,' she said. 'They sent her to the ovens.'

We sat at the kitchen table in silence. We sat till nightfall, thinking about Mamme and how safe we felt wrapped in her doughy, pale arms. And Tatte, clever, kind Tatte, who only wanted the best for us. And Willie: Willie walking me to school; Willie showing me a right hook; Willie making me laugh; Willie refusing to let the war and guards and hunger win.

I clung tight to my sisters in those first weeks of family, thankful to have them. I knew others who had fared worse, who had survived the camps to find their whole families extinguished—parents, siblings, cousins and aunts. But Mamme and Tatte were dead, and Willie too. Try as I did to anchor myself in family, I felt lost.

Rozsi and Cili stayed afloat by marrying, both opting for

older, wealthy, reliable husbands. Rozsi's Miksa was fourteen years her senior and had lost a wife and two children to the war. He was short, plump, balding and serious, a surprising match for my feisty, attractive sister, yet understandable, given the deprivations she had suffered in the concentration camps and the support and security she now craved. Cili, at seventeen, also chose safety, marrying Lajos, a solemn, religious man.

I stayed away from all things serious. I taught myself to ride a bike, made friends and went to my first wedding, where I drank too much and learnt how to flirt. There were so many weddings in 1946, so many people anxious to make up for lost time.

I was in no rush. I was sixteen and still discovering what it meant to be a survivor and an orphan. I'd lost my parents and my best friend, Willie. I didn't need to fall in love, I needed to heal myself.

Part of that healing was to continue my education, to reconstruct the man I hoped to be, the man Tatte and Mr Lukac knew I could be. I assumed my family would be supportive. School, my brothers-in-law told me, was out of the question. I was sixteen now, and responsible for my own survival. I needed to work to support myself. The only question was what form my employment should take. I settled on motor mechanics.

'Are you kidding?' Miksa asked.

'Just think about the filth and the grease. Impossible to get out from under your fingernails! You'll freeze in winter, lying under those cars, and in summer you'll sweat. That's no future. What you want is a nice heated room in winter and a fan to keep you cool in summer. What you'll do is become a jeweller. We're moving to Kosice. You can live with us.'

The decision was made. I didn't complain. I was a kid with no money and a limited education. I'd be lucky to get an apprenticeship, lucky to live with Rozsi and Miksa in a city rich enough to justify a jeweller's apprentice. I packed my bags and kissed Cili and Alex goodbye.

Within a week of arriving in Kosice I was employed as a jeweller's apprentice, had enrolled at night school, and secured a job on the side cleaning the boss's house and babysitting his children, Gita and Fredi. I thought that if I got up to speed, if I squeezed it all in, reclaimed all the years that Hitler had taken from me, the pain of those years might be negated, the loss and suffering cancelled out.

My days were spent polishing rings and my nights reading textbooks by torchlight under my blankets. I completed the equivalent of years nine, ten and eleven by my eighteenth birthday, with the help of a private tutor who, upon learning of my secret studies, donated his time free of charge. I planned to graduate high school the following year. I told none of this to my brother or sisters, who viewed intellectual pursuit as frivolity, the acquiring of knowledge a waste of time. My days were best served, they said, in a factory collecting paychecks. School just earned one degrees, bits of paper that were useless to the butcher and of no value to a landlord. What did I want with talk of the theatre, literature and music?

Everything, I wanted to say. I want it all. I want to learn

to play the piano, travel, read, study history.

'Enough with the reading!' my brother-in-law would curse, finding me hunched over the newspaper at night. 'You know how to read, Emil. For what do you need all these newspapers?'

I was a disappointment to my family, a boy who turned away from the past, from a life they were trying to recapture.

Kosice was a city of seventy thousand inhabitants. It boasted a large Jewish population and a dizzying array of activities for a young, impressionable village boy. Rozsi and Miksa suggested I find my way through the maze by joining a Jewish Youth Group. They hinted at Bnei Akiva, a religious Zionist youth movement. I wasn't yet reconciled with God and had no plans to resettle in Palestine, so chose instead to join Hashomer Hatzair. The left-wing socialist youth movement felt like a better fit, at least for a time. I learnt to play table-tennis and perform martial arts. I went to the theatre and hiked in the hills. I went to picnics and visited museums. The children at Hashi read books and went to galleries, they discussed art and debated politics. I borrowed their books and took them to my tutor.

'I want to know what they know. I need to catch up,' I told him.

My friends visited with copies of *Das Kapital* tucked under their arms. We discussed Marx and debated God's existence. My brother-in-law stood seething in a corner, furious.

'I don't want them here again. Not in my house,' Miksa thundered.

Rozsi took a softer approach. She knew the harder Miksa pushed, the more resolute I would be to see my

Thursday: Escape

friends. In an attempt to steer me back to their life and away from my new, irreligious, socialist-leaning youth group Rozsi introduced me to her friends. I declined all offers for Talmud study sessions and Friday-night prayer groups, but did make one friend, Aniko, their maid. Aniko was a wild-haired, plump country girl—and very friendly. We spent lazy afternoons together when the house had been emptied for work, or got together early while the house still slept. I didn't tell Rozsi that I'd been swept away by her maid; after all, Rozsi had hired Aniko to clean the kitchen table, not have sex on it.

Karl Marx wanted us to stay put and build socialism at home. I wanted to leave. He believed we should give according to our ability and take what we need. I wanted to work hard, keep what I made and make more. So I left the youth group. My entire wage had been divided among my friends, whereas the other youth group members—students who lived at home supported by their parents—only contributed pocket money. They spent their share of the kitty on galleries and picnics; I used mine to buy food and clothing. I was too poor to be a socialist.

Alex stayed in Velke Kapusany. He was busy with a new wife, Berta, a thriving textile business and an equally lucrative black-market trade in cigarettes. I helped out when I could, smuggling Russian cigarettes into Prague in return for accommodation in the city, a ticket to the circus and lunch. Alex showed me how to tie the brick-shaped cartons to my body, disguising my bulk under an oversized trenchcoat and loose baggy pants. I would walk from the station to the seediest part of town, to the dingiest flat, deliver the goods, pocket a sealed envelope and, kilos lighter, run for the circus to catch the next show.

Alex gave me a map, but I discovered the secrets of the city—its noise, colour and chaos—alone. I stumbled into dusty bookshops and gazed into dimly lit cafés. I fingered trinkets at market stalls and hiked to storybook castles. I wandered at dusk among Prague's dome-topped churches and crumbling chapels, maimed by Hitler but not destroyed. I ran my fingers along the bricked walls of spiky-topped cathedrals and majestic theatres, buildings designed for beauty, with arches and columns to please the eye. I had grown up with mud walls and straw roofs built to keep out the rain; later, barrack boxes housed me, sheets of corrugated iron and exposed nails. But nothing like this.

I saw the circus four times and then retired from the smuggling racket, a step closer to answering the nagging question of 'home'. Porubka had been a holding pattern. Now the whole country—even Prague—seemed like the wrong choice. My future was in a city, a noisy, thriving, thrumming place, but one untouched by death. A city still inventing its own history as I would invent mine. A young country across the sea: America.

I tried three separate American consular officials.

'Sorry son, only place you're going is with your sister,' they said.

Rozsi and Miksa had applied for residency in Palestine. I'd barely survived one war. Nothing could get me to Palestine to risk fighting another. Nor could I stay in Czechoslovakia with Cili or Alex. The communists had seized political power. Free elections were abolished; opposing political

Thursday: Escape

parties prohibited; private property, factories and businesses nationalised; and religion discouraged. It seemed to me a frightening echo of earlier times, so when a few days later Emanuel, a boy I had befriended in a soup kitchen, asked me to escape with him to Austria, I jumped at the chance. I was four months short of completing my apprenticeship and two months shy of my matriculation exams. It was April 1949.

I packed socks, underwear, two shirts and a pair of trousers into a rucksack and kissed Rozsi goodbye, gifting her, Cili and Alex my share of the Porubka estate. It wasn't hard to leave.

'Promise you'll call,' Cili cried into the phone. 'We don't want to lose you again.'

I left for the Slovakian capital Bratislava that day. Taking advantage of the deal struck between the provisional Israeli government and the Czech government to let Hungarian Jews pass unhindered into the American sector of Vienna, Emanuel and I registered on arrival as Hungarians. Happily forsaking our heritage and leaving behind our identification papers, we smuggled ourselves aboard a late-night train bound for Vienna. We arrived at the station three hours later. Two American army trucks laid in wait. We scrambled onto them and sat hunched and silent on the floor of the truck until we reached Arzburger.

Tucked into the American-controlled section of Vienna, Arzberger transit home for refugees was a home resembling the concentration camp-style barracks of my youth—bunk beds for two hundred in a shared living space. But here people argued, fought and made love without fear of punishment. Here my stomach was full. I made sure not to wander off the grounds and stray into the Russian Zone, where it was rumoured the boy who had slept on my bunk before me had been intercepted, before being taken to Siberia.

I waited a week before contacting Cili, remaining vague about my whereabouts. I knew the communist authorities were in the habit of intercepting mail. I thought if Cili were ignorant of my address, she would be spared. Instead the party chose to punish her for my defection, refusing to grant her a passport to travel, the freedom to leave.

After what felt like an eternity, but was perhaps no more than six days, I crept aboard a midnight truck and, camouflaged by night, using back roads, the American army ferried me to my next home. Emanuel did not accompany me. He had snuck away the night before, to join an uncle with residency permits for Canada. I was alone but unafraid. I had money in my pocket—Austrian shillings from Jewish Welfare, and two gold coins from Aunt Merele. I was on my way to America.

Styer, a refugee camp in the American zone of Austria, housed predominantly Jewish refugees fleeing communism. I listened and learned and soon found out that my chances for passage to America were better at Ebelsberg, a refugee camp on the outskirts of the neighbouring town of Linz. A Canadian lady, a Mrs Weston, would be in Ebelsberg later that week to see whether there were any children there who might qualify for placement in her YMCA home. Though at Styer I shared a large room with only two other boys, though we were free to wander Styer's narrow cobbled streets and cool our toes in the rushing waters of its river, with the Alps as a backdrop, I was ready for the move. I liked the idea of a

Thursday: Escape

home for boys: it conjured up images of ball games, bonfires and midnight feasts, images gleaned from the English children's books I'd borrowed from the Kosice school library. And it was rumoured to be a fast-track to America.

I was first in line for the interviews. I'd prepared myself for a grilling, imagining my inquisitor as a towering, glaring hulk of a woman in a pin-striped suit, scratching answers on a black clipboard, a ream of paper choked with questions spilling from her briefcase. I was wrong. Mrs Weston was blonde and wore a wide grin and tailored slacks. She pulled up a chair and shook my hand.

'Want a Coke?' she offered, smiling.

She asked to hear my story and I talked for an hour in my best broken English. She held my hand and invited me to stay at St Gilgen, in her home for boys. 'Just until you make it to America with the help of the Hebrew Immigrant Aid Society office in Paris.'

I told her that I'd already applied, but that the office had rejected my application because my sister was off to Palestine and I was over eighteen.

'Apply again, then,' she suggested. 'This time you'll be sixteen and you'll have my backing. I'll collect you in two weeks.'

I returned to Styer with instructions to obtain new identity papers and an apprenticeship certificate. That meant finding witnesses to testify that I was sixteen, and sitting exams. The first task proved easier than I'd anticipated, due to a chance meeting two days later with an old friend of Tatte's, Ludevit Ehrenreich. Ludevit, sensing the urgency of my request, organised a second witness that day, and together they gifted me my new birthday, 10 September 1932. I received my identity papers three days later. To earn the apprenticeship certificate I had to pass practical and written exams at the Linz Technical School. A floral-design synthetic-ruby pendant satisfied the practical requirement and, two cups of coffee later, I passed the written examination, returning to collect my jeweller's diploma the day before Mrs Weston's arrival.

She came for me in a three-piece suit, in a chauffeur-driven, shiny black car. I waved goodbye to my bug-eyed campmates, tossed my bag into the boot and sank into the doughy softness of the leather bucket-seat beside her.

St Gilgen was far more beautiful than I'd ever imagined. A grand old house, crumbling but still magical, it was set in a huge garden on the edge of glassy blue Lake Wolfgang. I shared a bedroom with twenty-five others, thirteen sets of bunks fanned out around the perimeter of our room with space in the middle for cartwheels, card games and friendly wrestling matches. At night the boys would drag their blankets to the middle of the room and tell fantastic war stories, each trying to outdo the storyteller before him with wild tales of heroic deeds and daring escapes. We all knew Marti hadn't smuggled grenades into Germany and that Peter wasn't responsible for the escape of forty-five Jews from Dachau, but still we listened.

I woke each morning to a bright, clear sky and the sound of boots chasing balls across muddied lawns. I rowed

Thursday: Escape

through the still lake and swam when the sun shone. I ate three meals a day in an oak-panelled dining room at a long wooden table. I ate alone surrounded by other people's friendships. My housemates came from Poland, Yugoslavia, Romania, Hungary and Czechoslovakia. Of St Gilgen's one hundred residents, only seven were Jews, and although Jew and gentile shared a common aim—that of escaping communism—somehow a line had been drawn. I was still an outsider, permitted to watch the fun and games, but not invited to play.

Determining who was Jewish was a delicate task. I noticed Berti on my first day at St Gilgen. He was telling a story, his exaggerated airs, laughing smile and sparkling eyes tempting gentile attention. I wanted this smiling, cocky, dark-haired kid to be Jewish; I wanted to be his friend.

I approached him one night after dinner, speaking to him in the Hungarian I'd heard him use with his friends.

'You're Jewish, aren't you?' I ventured.

'Yes, I am. I'm Berti Burger. I'm seventeen, and on my way to Australia. What about you?'

'I'm Emil,' I answered, 'and I'm as far off seventeen as you are. Only difference is, I look seventeen. You look closer to twenty-five.'

I was spot on, about the age and our friendship.

Berti liked to box. I preferred table-tennis, so I joined St Gilgen's table-tennis team, lifting them for the first time from the bottom of the ladder. It was a tough season for the team, who wanted the new member—the Jew—to lose, but also wanted the trophy in equal measure. I was playing in the final; the score was eight–all. I could hear Berti to my left cheering madly and losing his voice and the rest of St Gilgen, unconflicted, cheering on our opposition. At fifteen–all Berti signalled for play to stop. He rose from his seat, red-faced, and turned to our housemates. Nickolae sat behind him. Nick was Bert's best friend, a six-foot three, two-hundred-pound amateur boxer.

Berti approached the most vocal cheerleader, a St Gilgen boy, a doubles player on my team.

'Listen, you,' he said reaching up to grab the boy by the collar. 'Emil is playing for the honour of this house. Your house. One more sound out of you and this fist,' he said, flailing his meaty arm around, 'will go through your nose to the other side of your head.'

The boy, a head taller than Berti and twice as wide, lunged for the flying fist, hissing, 'You and what army, tough guy?'

To which Nick, stepping out from Bert's shadow answered, 'This army.'

I resumed play to a vocal audience of seven. The rest of the hall was too stunned to speak. Now the match favourite, I powered to victory, winning twenty-one–seventeen to take home the trophy.

Unfortunately, Big Nick couldn't always be there to shield me from prejudice. He couldn't force my housemates to like me, though he tried—first with gentle persuasion, later with blows. I was a Jew, so they wouldn't let themselves get to know me. Were they scared of what they might discover? That I was a boy just like them, just as alone, equally daring? Someone they might like?

Perhaps if they'd gotten to know me, they wouldn't have laughed and rowed on as I struggled five miles along

Thursday: Escape

a swirling Lake Wolfgang in a damaged canoe. I'd made the four-hour trip to the White Horse Inn, only to be refused entrance to the café. My housemates had sneered from the balcony and later, after a storm had blown up and damaged my vessel, had sailed past me for home, making no effort to mask their pleasure at the prospect of my drowning.

I applied to the HIAS office in Paris for passage to America and waited.

※

In September 1949 the lease on St Gilgen expired. The new landlord gave us two weeks to find new lodgings. It was ample time to pack our meagre belongings, but not nearly enough time to say goodbye. I had become part of a group—the Jews and Nick, small but tight. There were times we had been safe, mainly when in Big Nick's presence, times when nobody abused us, when we spent hours hiking in the countryside or splashing in the lake. Good times. A taste of the future. Now Berti was leaving for Australia without a forwarding address.

I moved on to Camp Hellbrun in Salzburg. Impersonal, cold, and run with military precision, the refugee camp was not a home, but a roof over my head. I missed my cosy room, the midnight storytelling, the intimacy of the dining room. I missed Berti, Nick and the gang of boys I had come to call family. I missed Mrs Weston. I managed because I spoke German. My years spent eavesdropping on my parents' Yiddish conversations had lent me some fluency in my host country's tongue. I acted as translator and spokesman for my housemates, and so spent little time alone.

One Sunday a group of us from Hellbrun decided to visit the cinema. After queuing for an hour, we were one man shy of the box office when a group of pimply teenagers stepped in front of my friend Eugene.

'Bloody foreigners, get to the back of the queue,' was all they said, all they believed needed saying, given our race.

'*You* get to the end of the queue,' I shouted, pushing to the front, stepping up to the ticket office. In the beginning, when I first arrived at Hellbrun, when I was first forced to speak for my housemates, to act the leader because I spoke German, I pretended bravery. But within weeks I found myself wanting to speak up, unable to do anything but speak out. Eugene, who had followed me from St Gilgen to Hellbrun, put his hands over my fists.

'Emil, we'd all like to fight,' he pretended, 'but a fight will only jeopardise our passage to America. We're the ones who will get locked up.'

I knew Eugene was right, but it hurt to walk away, to let them have our seats.

I got my revenge in ways that, looking back, seem silly: using my flair for German to gain entry to restaurants closed to Jews, making the gentile refugees beg me to act as their translator. These small victories returned to me the power I'd surrendered as a child.

❦

I'd been in Salzburg for two months when the Berlin blockade started. With the Allies refused access to Berlin by road, tensions mounted. In the hallways at Hellbrun, talk

Thursday: Escape

was of a Third World War. I had to get out of Europe, fast. If the United States wouldn't have me, I reasoned, I'd just have to find a country that would. Canada rejected me for being too small, South America wasn't interested. I'd never thought about Australia. All I knew of the country was that it was large, far away and populated by kangaroos. I learnt they were looking for migrants. Would Australia make a good home? I wondered. It was remote and therefore less likely to be attacked in the event of war. It was a young country with a bright future, willing to have a skinny, bespeckled Jew as a citizen. It was perfect, I convinced myself, as I headed to the Australian consulate.

The consular official, a burly, sandy-haired fellow, placed a two-year contract on the desk in front of me.

'Sit down, mate, and I'll translate the mumbo-jumbo,' the young man offered. I had no idea what he'd just said, so I smiled.

He continued, this time speaking very slowly and very loudly. 'We'll let you in if you agree to work for the Australian government for two years at any job anywhere in the country we determine. How does that sound?'

I signed immediately.

Two weeks later I was on a train bound for Naples. I couldn't sit still. Since choosing my new home, I'd found out more about Australia. I now knew the girls were blonde, tanned, and keen for dark, handsome European men. The beaches were covered with the softest white sand, and money could be made, lots of it, if you were prepared to work hard. I paced the length of the train, playing imaginary home movies in my head, where I owned my own home, ran my own business and had three laughing, blond-haired, blue-eyed kids who looked just like their mother.

I chose the boys I approached for information as I had chosen my friends at St Gilgen, hoping they were Jewish and that friendship might follow. Eugene was seated beside me on the train and would follow me to Australia, but we weren't kindred spirits. We lived life too differently. Eugene lived defensively, to survive. I wanted to experience life to grow. I knew his negativity stemmed from a profound sense of inferiority and I tried to build him up, to stem the whining, to whip up some enthusiasm, but I failed. I wanted friends who would fan my excitement, not temper it.

I approached two boys, asking if they knew of our arrival time. The elder of the two, an olive-skinned fellow with strong, even features lifted his face from behind a newspaper. 'Four hours left to go,' he smiled, pushing up his wire-rimmed spectacles.

'And then a fortnight in Naples, and a month on board a ship. You're heading to Australia, too, aren't you?' asked the second boy, before introducing himself. 'I'm Louis Adler and this is my brother Andrew.'

We shook hands and Andrew went back to his paper. Louis and I exchanged histories. He had survived forced labour camps and a stint at Mauthausen. His parents, killed in the camps, had run a general store and he'd returned home to Hungary with his brother to reclaim it. Both found communism abhorrent and had escaped while there was still time. We'd all been to Linz, had all been smuggled on American transports to Styer, and were all bound for Melbourne.

Thursday: Escape

We were taken from the train directly to an army barracks in the suburb of Bagnoli. Louis threw his bag onto the stretcher bed nearest mine, Andrew ditched his books and, ignoring the camp commandant's order not to leave the barracks, we jumped the fence and headed to Pompeii. We toured the ruins, wondering aloud what our towns looked like now, overrun with communism. We walked among Bagnoli's orange groves, and tasted our first orange. We watched Vesuvius smoking in the distance. We ate pasta and drank red wine. Louis and Andrew had money tucked away from the sale of their parents' home and general store. They had a diamond embedded in a bridge in Louis' mouth. I left the continent penniless, armed with but a few fond memories.

I stood on the dock at the Bay of Naples, my mouth hanging open. A ship, a gleaming grey vessel, taller than any building I'd ever seen and wider than any city street, loomed in front of me. Beyond it lay the bay: my first glimpse of open water, blue as far as the eye could see. Louis pointed up at the black letters painted along the ship's flank.

'The *General W. C. Langfitt*,' I said. 'Our home for the next thirty-two days.'

We stood there for a while, marvelling at the water, and then climbed aboard. Two other Jewish boys I'd met in transit, Philip Spiegel and Louis Kornfeld, joined Louis, Andrew, Eugene and me, and once again, I was part of a group. Poor Kornfeld made the mistake of admitting he couldn't stand ship travel. His premature panic attacks and constant whining steeled our resolve to test his neuroses. With the ship still tied to the wharf, I approached Kornfeld and shook his hand.

'Good on you, Kornfeld. You're a real trooper,' I said borrowing the slang of the army personnel on board. 'It's been hours now that we've been at sea, and look how well you're coping. Not a hint of sea sickness.'

Within seconds Kornfeld had thrown up over his shoes. By the end of the trip, there wasn't a deck he hadn't sullied with his half-digested meals. Eventually, he gave up eating altogether, dropping two trouser sizes, and seeing me, the benefactor of his missed meals, gain four kilos.

I shared a hold with Kornfeld, Phillip and six-hundred-and-ninety-seven others, sleeping in four-tiered bunk beds. Another fourteen hundred refugees slept alongside us in the ship's two other holds. I heard there were American marines on board, sleeping in separate quarters, but I rarely saw them. Being a US Army troop-carrier, the ship was run with military precision. We woke, ate and retired to our rooms at exactly the same time each day. Only our rostered hours of work varied.

My job on board was relaying the public announcements. I got the job after adding 'Polish' to the line-up of four languages boasted by the applicant before me. In reality he spoke Polish every bit as well as I did; it was just our interpretation of the word 'fluent' that differed. I also served as interpreter in the ship's supply shop, garnering me immediate popularity, given my perceived control over cigarette rationing. Unfortunately my popularity didn't extend to the ship's female population who informed me they preferred more mature company such as Louis'. While Andrew's nose was buried in books, his little brother was charming the female population on board. He was also popular with the boys, emerging from the storeroom in which he worked with pockets bulging with apples, oranges and cans of tomato juice, which he distributed freely. I'd never tasted tomato juice before. I drank cans of the stuff. And devoured oranges, peeling one after the other and sucking the sweet juice from their skins. Louis also provided a regular supply of onions which I cut into quarters and rubbed over Kornfeld's body to alleviate his eczema. Our room-mates held their nose every time they entered our hold.

This must be how it feels to be on a first-class cruise, I imagined, ignoring the stench and overcrowding: plenty of food, great company, balmy nights and a wonderful, mysterious destination. It was all we could talk of—our new home and the wonderful, exciting, successful lives we'd lead. We argued about religion. Although I still wrestled with the concept of God's existence, I still felt very much a Jew. Not because I'd survived the death march, been transported by cattle train or been branded by tattoo. All those mornings in Shul with Tatte, baking *challah* with Mamme, studying the Talmud for Wasserman—that's what being a Jew meant. It was more about home than about the deity; he was still on probation. I would continue to attend synagogue in Australia, I swore to myself, because that's where I'd find my parents and Willie. Once a year on Yom Kippur I would say *kaddish* (prayers for the dead) with a rabbi, because that was how Tatte had honoured the dead, and how Tatte would have wanted to be honoured.

More turned *from* God than to him. Murder had cancelled out faith. Others turned from religion because a fresh start demanded it. A vocal minority held fast to their faith. To them, my vow to find God once a year to pray for dead relatives was an insultingly inadequate show of faith to a God who had called an end to the madness.

There was room for us all, believers and heretics.

Thirteen

APRIL 2002

'I want to die on a Friday,' he tells us. The significance of this day eludes me, but the significance of this moment, this meeting, does not.

My father sits in his high-back, black leather swivel chair, still calling the shots.

'That way, the funeral will be on the weekend and no one has to miss work.'

My father attempts a smile. I try not to cry.

Dad keeps typing, though I can see he is exhausted. Not from the emotional strain of directing his death, but from the Herculean effort it takes to raise his last functioning finger to the keyboard. We wait in silence. And then he speaks again, in his new voice, his American-accented computer-generated voice. The unwavering tones of the LightWriter 2000.

'I've paid for a double plot. Make sure I'm buried on the right, like we lie in bed.'

He turns to my mother. 'This is one time I don't want you to come to bed early.'

Bubbles of sweat ring his brow. His breathing is fast and laboured.

'I want you to be happy, Judy,' the machine intones. No undertone of grief. 'I want you to travel, work and meet a man.'

My mother cries and runs to hug her husband. Not to thank him for the generous gift of freeing her to be happy, but to whisper dangerous promises in his ear. I hear her words and despair for her.

He battles on. 'I want you all to be happy. Stay close to one another and look out for each other. Mourn as you need to, but live your lives.'

The instructions continue for an hour, at the end of which he asks my brother Gary, who has been taking notes, to read back his wishes. I listen again to talk of wills and investments, burial rites and medical intervention. Only now, when his final wishes are repeated back to him in the very human, very shaky voice of his son, does my father allow a tear to escape. My mother reaches for a tissue but she can't wipe away the sadness.

We arrive at the big question that no one wants to ask. I break the silence with a whisper.

'When will it be enough, Dad?'

I can't look my father in the eye. I feel that by asking the question I'm inviting death in.

My father presses a single button, retrieving a pre-recorded message. He's thought about this, about a time in the future when his fingers will be too weak to tap at his LightWriter.

'I'll let you know when I'm ready. I'll blink once for yes and twice for no.'

April 2002

My mother jumps to her feet, rushing to erase his words.
'I can't do it, Emil. I won't.'

They argue and she negotiates a painful compromise. The ventilator will be switched off only if my father is insistent for a continuous period of seven days.

He makes us give our word. I write the code down—once for yes, twice for no—in black ink on a notepad and carry it over to my father. He touches his tongue to the roof of his mouth and draws it away sharply, making a clicking sound, which in this instance I take as approval.

One click, delivered slowly. It's a language. His language. One sound capable of expressing a dozen emotions. Anger: a round of clicks fired off at increasing volume, much like a shotgun. A cry for help: slow, loud and repetitive. Thankful: one click, blown soft and full, like a kiss. He tilts his head and motions towards my brothers, and I pass the page to each, in turn. We repeat the instructions out loud and in unison until my father signals his satisfaction.

It's his incredible strength that stays with me and sustains me three weeks later in the labour ward, allowing me to deliver an eight-pound baby girl without drugs.

'You call that pain?' I imagine my father calling in response to my first contraction. I visualise my father hovering behind the midwives and I have to agree. Compared to his pain, constant and unrelenting—a pain capable of being cut short only by death—these contractions are nothing. So I breathe through them, smiling at the picture in my head.

An hour later the pain is worse, the contractions more intense. Comparisons offer no comfort. I want out.

'Where's the fucking epidural??' I yell at the walls, squeezing my eyes shut. But instead of expelling the pain, I find a tunnel. I fumble through, in the dark, towards a voice. It's my father calling me to join him at the other end.

'You can do it, Suzy,' he tells me, and I know he's right. I grab his outstretched arm and he pulls me from the dark, out of the contractions, away from the pain.

I replay this scenario, over and over, through a hundred contractions, until I hear the midwife tell me to push. My father disappears as my third child slides from me into life.

Mum rolls Dad's wheelchair to my bedside in the delivery suite two hours later. We cry when we see each other. All I can say is 'thank you'.

I look at my daughter, puffy-eyed and floppy and sweet, thrown headfirst into life, and then at my father, equally dependent, thrust without his permission towards death.

The nurses step around my father's wheelchair cautiously, their eyes averted. My obstetrician stops momentarily at the doorway, caught off-guard by the scene: a family celebrating a new life, unfazed by the whirr of the electric suctioning device drawing phlegm from a tube embedded in my father's throat.

When did dying become normal for us? When did sputum and sweat and plastic tubing stop being frightening? Probably the first time my father asked me to wipe saliva from his lips. He wasn't embarrassed. He just needed looking after. It was normal because he made it normal.

'Come in,' Mum smiles at my obstetrician, forcing the doctor into our world. Making it normal for her, too. Rendering exclusion and ignorance unacceptable.

Fourteen

FRIDAY: THE NEW AUSTRALIAN

We docked at Port Melbourne on 14 January 1950. I'd been on deck since daybreak, searching for shore. The creatures on dry land were pinpricks at first, scurrying ants; then, as we got closer, I could make out windswept hair, sunburnt faces: Australians. Waving, grabbing at bags, loading trolleys, holding signs, smiling. Pot-bellied men in white singlets and khaki shorts with handkerchiefs tied to their heads loaded cargo onto trucks. Policemen stopped passengers and made small talk while checking identification. Customs officers asked kindly if we would please dispose of our fruit. Fishermen showed off hauls, and hawkers offered chocolate, cheese and girlie magazines. The air smelt of fish, stale tobacco and sweat. People looked happy.

It was like I'd been living underground and was finally let outdoors to feel the warmth of the sun and to see colour for the first time.

'I've found it,' I said to Louis. 'I've found my future.'

I stepped off the boat.

'God, I'd love a chocolate bar.'

'So have one. Here, take a shilling,' Andrew pressed a coin into my palm and I ran for the chocolate vendor.

'G'day, mate,' the freckle-faced boy smiled, holding out a dozen cellophane-wrapped bags.

'If you're here to sweeten your day you've come to the right place. So, what'll it be? Choc-nut, honeycomb, Turkish delight? They're all going cheap.' The boy was sweating from the midday heat. So were his chocolates.

I stood there, transfixed by his gap-toothed grin, his good-natured banter. This was an Australian, a kid who had grown up on beaches and pineapple juice, a thousand miles from hunger and hatred.

I looked around me. These people were good people, contented people. A nation eager for more people, people like me, to come live with them.

'Here, take a choc-nut then. Take two. Just don't hang on to them too long or they'll start to melt.' The boy prised the coin from my palm, winked and moved on.

I thought of home, of the kids who had thrown stones at me, the guards eager to unleash their dogs. It had been a bad time, and the ignorant and the angry had got caught up in it. Zosia hadn't, Mr Lukac hadn't. There had been good people, kind people. Here there were good people, too; I could sense it. The Holocaust had been an aberration — a dark, bleak time in history. It didn't define humanity and it wouldn't define me.

Two hours after our ship berthed, and only minutes after Kornfeld's stomach had finally settled, we boarded a train for the eight-hour trip to the Bonegilla migrant camp. I'd never sat in a train compartment before, on a seat near a window. I'd stood beside eighty others in a darkened cattle train. After the war I'd crouched on the roof of a train and ducked tunnels, but never once had I sat on leather. The countryside, it was true, was brown and burnt and the summer heat more oppressive than anything I'd known in Porubka. Carcasses of dead cows studded the landscape, and withered trees bowed to the sun. Still, its rawness appealed to me—the endless flat fields, the intensity of the sky. It was new, and for that I was thankful.

The faces of many of my shipmates fell when they saw the Bonegilla Reception Centre. Italians gestured wildly, Germans protested, the Dutch looked aghast. They saw flat, barren ground, rows of tin sheds, poky windows, toilet blocks, wash sheds and a kitchen block. Louis, Andrew and I surveyed our surroundings and saw a welcome banner flapping in the hot summer wind. We saw strange grey gum trees and unfamiliar eucalypts and, stepping into our barrack, a big room with just thirty beds, single beds with clean white sheets, thick, warm blankets and a set of drawers.

The other men whispered to each other, disgusted by the pits that served as toilets, frightened by the squawking of the magpie, wary of the ants crawling up the legs of their beds. We swatted at flies and trampled spiders and laughed at the newness of it all.

A voice over a loudspeaker announced the commencement of dinner and we filed into a larger hut with a corrugated iron roof for cold sliced lamb, peas and gravy — and a talking-to by a man introduced to us as the camp commander. I tried to translate the rules for Louis and the others, but in the end thought better of it. We wouldn't stick to them anyway.

We fell asleep late, after having finally removed two possums from the dormitory, and woke early to the strains of 'God Save the King'. Louis refused to leave the hut until I'd checked outside for wild animals.

'It was a bird. The strangest-looking thing. And that noise you heard, that was the bird's song. It's called a kookaburra,' I laughed.

We downed sausages and eggs for breakfast and lined up, as instructed, to collect our weekly stipend of two shillings. I took my brown paper bag rattling with change and lined up again, this time for the camp nurse.

'You, too?' she said, after I'd taken off my shirt and she saw my number, A7639.

'Yes,' I said, before changing the topic. 'So, I am fit to work?'

We spent the rest of the morning roaming the streets of surrounding Bonegilla. The locals called it 'Little Europe' but I was glad to see it was nothing like my hometown. There was a hospital, theatre, church and school, a canteen, a bank and a library. I ate my first pineapple and borrowed a book on Australian wildlife.

After lunch, we stripped off our clothes, wrapped our bath towels around us, and headed for the Hume Weir. The thirty-minute walk took us past farmers tending their sheep; a large hotel from which men stumbled, smelling of beer; and a small shop called a milk bar, which sold all sorts of wonderful sweets in addition to bottles of milk. I soon spent my silver on lemon squash and ice-cream.

'This Peter, whoever he is, sure makes a good vanilla cone,' I laughed, in between mouthfuls.

Weeks passed, each day a repeat of the one before. We would wake to the loudspeaker playing the British national anthem, spend our mornings splashing about in the cool waters of the Hume Weir or sleeping on the sand, and our afternoons playing soccer or table-tennis, or lazing on our beds. A few of the boys from St Gilgen, the same men who had taunted me for being Jewish, now played and laughed alongside me. We were all starting afresh. The line between Jew and non-Jew blurred. Prejudices fell away and labels shifted. We were all new Australians.

Sometimes we would walk through the open paddocks flanking the camp and lie in the dry, yellow grass, making grand plans for the future. Sometimes we'd chase rabbits. And every evening, before dinner, Louis and Andrew, Kornfeld and Philip would take their turns in the 'job placement office'. Eugene and I were too young to be placed.

'Louis Adler to the office,' the loudspeaker would drone, and I wished it were me. Louis and Andrew would return from the office with the same story each day.

'The career officer pointed to the map of Victoria and, again, his finger was nowhere near Melbourne,' said Louis. 'I told him, "I'll be a farmhand, I'll be a labourer, I'll work in a factory. I'll do anything you say, as long as the job is in Melbourne".'

Louis' mind was made up. He was not going back to a village life.

Friday: The New Australian

I just wanted to work.

Louis called a meeting of the Jewish contingent. 'I know we've signed a contract, but we aren't going to let a bit of paper hold us back, are we?' he said.

It took fourteen of us only twenty minutes to come up with a plan: we couldn't work for the businesses selected for us by the government because those jobs demanded a six-day work week. As Jews, we were bound to observe the Sabbath — Saturday was our day of rest.

'Australians rest on Sunday,' Eugene informed us, 'and I think they like to stick to the rules here.'

It was decided we would seek support from the Melbourne Jewish community. A delegation was to be sent to Melbourne and I was appointed delegate, being the only one who knew enough English to argue our cause.

'He's the youngest, barely out of nappies. He can't go alone. Not with my money,' one of the group chimed in.

'So send a chaperone,' Louis joked.

Which they did. 'The chief' was wide and strong as a bull, with a mouth as filthy. He had been a farmer and landowner in Hungary, and was happy for the opportunity to escape his new job as foreman of the toilet block at Bonegilla, even if for only a few days. As well as being twice my size, the chief was twice my age and therefore deemed trustworthy with the £13 we'd scrounged together that would have to see us through two nights in Melbourne. I was spokesman but agreed the chief would call the shots — at least that's what I'd let him think he was doing. His first decision, I intimated, should be to jump on a bus to Wodonga and from there board a train to Melbourne.

I nudged the chief awake at Spencer Street Station, suggesting we head up Bourke Street in search of a synagogue, a kosher butcher, or a store bearing a Jewish name. Eventually, I reasoned, we'd find a tailor by the name of Rosenblum, or a merchant with a *mezuzah* on his door. There were lots of stores that, like Tatte's, sold all manner of goods — shoes and chocolates and books and linen — but they were ten times the size of Tatte's store, and none of them had a *mezuzah* on its door.

'So what do you think, smart guy? Are Misters Buckley and Nunn or Foy and Gibson gonna help us Jewish boys?'

I kept walking. Two blocks further on I found a phone booth with a thick yellow directory listing all Melbourne businesses, associations and establishments. I looked up 'Jewish'.

No entries, so I turned to 'H' for 'Hebrew'. The chief, who had been complaining of sore feet, brightened when I pointed out there was a Hebrew Congregation of Melbourne in the suburb of South Yarra. A short ride later on a rattling timber tram and we were in Toorak Road. The synagogue loomed overhead, a massive building topped with a glistening green dome. Further down the street stood rows of fine homes with carefully tended gardens. I ran up the steps and pushed open the heavy double doors. It was cool, quiet and dark inside.

'I'm sorry, the rabbi is not in,' his secretary informed us. 'He's at home and not to be disturbed.'

The chief turned to go, but I held him back.

'Give me a minute,' I said, hurrying after the secretary, determined not to give up at the first hurdle. I knew the power of my story and when to use it. I used it on the rabbi's secretary who, at the end of my tale, pressed a piece of paper into my palm. It was a short walk down St Kilda Road to the rabbi's address, but I walked slowly, mesmerised by the gliding trams, the endless sweep of the street and the total absence of litter. I stopped at a towering silver building to count the floors.

'Eleven!' I told the chief, but he didn't seem interested. The men and women who entered and exited their grand homes in three-piece suits and starched white shirts were just as perfectly manicured as the nature strip. I was a little disappointed that I hadn't seen a kangaroo or koala; but, all in all, I was convinced that in Melbourne I'd found the world's most beautiful city.

The rabbi was not happy to see us. Even my sad plight, recounted to him in his mother tongue for extra affect, did little to tweak his sympathy. I guessed pretty quickly that if the rabbi hadn't offered us a glass of water on this stinking hot summer's day, he wasn't going to offer a solution to our work situation. The rabbi heaved himself out of his chair and motioned us to the door.

'Try the Kadimah in Carlton,' he offered. 'Perhaps they'll help.'

We caught the number sixteen tram to Lygon Street and hopped off at Fenwick Street. I checked the address the rabbi had given me. The Kadimah was an imposing building, with its arched windows and columned foyer, but it housed a Yiddish theatre, community hall and Jewish library, not the welfare organisation I had hoped for.

'At least the rabbi wanted us entertained,' I joked. The

chief didn't appreciate the humour, or perhaps he just didn't feel like laughing. It was forty degrees out and he was developing blisters on his feet. The girl at the bar offered us a drink. The chief motioned towards the Scotch, but I was spokesman so we got water. I didn't know how long we'd be staying in Melbourne; we'd already spent £2 on transport, and I wasn't going to spend any more. Not until we'd found a room for the night.

It was past five by now and Melbourne was shutting down. We walked the streets of Carlton, and passed men with long beards on their way to synagogue and children in skullcaps playing soccer in the street. We saw kosher butchers close up shop and bakers sell the last of their bagels. Even across the sea, the Jews had made a corner for themselves. They had escaped annihilation and set themselves up again in streets named Drummond and Rathdowne. I made a mental note of my bearings. Louis would want directions.

The chief tried to use his man-in-charge status to pressure me into staying at a fancy hotel. His talk of gourmet meals and soft downy quilts, room service and warm baths was tempting.

'It would be our little secret, just for one night,' he whispered, following me through laneways and darkened alleys, finally falling silent at the doorway of a Salvation Army shelter, a tip from the barmaid. We shared a plate of sandwiches for dinner but little conversation; the chief was angry.

Next morning we set off for the Victorian Children's Welfare Department. A Jewish woman introduced herself as Marion and ushered us in. She would oversee our case, she advised, and wanted to hear my story, from the start, from Porubka.

'I'm sorry,' she said to the chief at the end of my story. 'You've signed a contract. There's nothing the Department can do for you.'

Then she turned to me.

'Can we talk?' she asked. 'Privately?'

The Jewish Welfare Society, Marion explained, brought under-age orphans out from Europe from time to time. They found guardians for the children and set them up in Melbourne. If I wrote to them, she assured me, Eugene and I, being teenagers, could be out of Bonegilla within a fortnight. I took her phone number and promised to keep in touch.

We returned to Bonegilla two days later, our mission a failure. I never spoke of the Jewish Welfare scheme, not to the group or to Eugene. I'd travelled to Melbourne at the group's behest. It didn't feel right to return with a release for two.

Over the next four months, each member of our group, save for Eugene and me, was assigned a job outside Bonegilla. Kornfeld and Philip didn't make it as far as Melbourne, but they were earning money and a degree of independence in nearby Albury. The Adler brothers had finally agreed to work in Upper Ferntree Gully. It was as close as they were going to get to Melbourne, advised the exasperated employment officer.

'What will you do? I asked Louis as he packed his bags to leave.

'I don't know. "Something with pebbles", the man said. "Quarrying", I think he called it.'

I handed Louis a banana and a slice of pineapple filched

from the breakfast table, and shook his hand.

'I'll be seeing you in Melbourne, then,' I said.

I was dying to work, to get out among real Australians, but I was considered too young for quarrying and road-building, and too old to be sent to school, so I stayed on at Bonegilla, assigned to rubbish duty. It was like entering a race and being held back at the starting line. I couldn't stand it, so I took matters into my own hands and went to Albury. Every second shopfront and factory had a 'wanted: worker' sign tacked to its window. I walked straight past cafés and milk bars, Art Deco buildings and Victorian terraces. I didn't stop to chat with the smiling usherettes dressed in full-length gowns advertising the latest double feature at the Albury cinema or accept a free lunch from the Good Neighbour Council. I stopped only to duck into factories and enquire about wages. By four o'clock I'd found a job at the Albury Sheepskin Factory, reporting the following day for work with Eugene. In ill-fitting, putrid-smelling overalls, we dipped our brushes into potent chemicals and spent one day painting sheepskin hides and the next pulling the wool off the sheepskin. The stench was horrible, but the money was good, so we stuck at it.

As the coins grew heavy in my pocket and the thrill of earning a dollar any way, anywhere, faded, I found myself dreaming of Melbourne. I called a meeting of the youth contingent at Bonegilla, and together the twenty of us resolved to ask the camp commander for our immediate release. I was elected spokesman and literally pushed forward into the office. Eugene and the others stood behind me, half in, half out the door. I cleared my throat.

'There are many young men in Bonegilla and we want to leave, Sir, as soon as it is possible, to make a life in Melbourne, Sir,' I stammered in halting English.

'Step forward, boy!' boomed the commander. My mates crept backwards, out the door, leaving me all alone to face his rage.

'You ungrateful shit,' he yelled, his mouth so close to mine I could smell his breakfast. 'We bring you out here to this beautiful country from starving Europe where you lived off the smell of an oily rag, and what do you become? You become a rabble-rouser and a troublemaker. One more squeak out of you and you'll be on the next ship back to where you came from.'

I nearly shat my pants. Back to Europe?

'No, Sir, you misunderstand,' I backtracked, begging his forgiveness, swearing undying allegiance to his King and country. 'I love Australia. Please do not send me back.'

The commander relented. 'Okay. You can stay. For now. But one more outburst and you're gone!'

I slunk out the door, a marked man.

I had to get out of Bonegilla fast. I was by nature rebellious and I knew it was just a matter of time before I was caught again doing something to upset the authorities. It was time to go, time to call Marion and accept her offer to live in Melbourne. I eased my guilt by reminding myself that the other boys had work—under contract—but work just the same. It still felt wrong, though, to accept Marion's short-cut while Louis and the others did time. Tatte wouldn't approve; he always put the community first. I had to accept that, in some ways, I wasn't my old man. It didn't feel good.

It took Eugene some time to get over the fact that I hadn't gotten him out of Bonegilla earlier. By the time he was talking to me again, it was the winter of 1950. He would continue talking to me, he advised, on condition that I write to the Jewish Welfare Society and secure our immediate release. Huddled under my one woollen blanket I composed the long overdue letter.

A few days later we heard from Marion. The Welfare Society was on our case and once they had found guardians, her note read, it should be relatively easy to convince the Minister for Social Welfare to release us from our contractual obligations. The only hitch was that the government had to be satisfied, in writing, that our guardians were able to take full financial responsibility for us; we were not to be left in a position where a request might be made for a government handout.

The Welfare Society worked fast, and by the end of July Eugene and I were living in the leafy, elegant suburb of Camberwell in one of the society's six welfare homes. Ten families shared the old two-storey mansion with us, but no one ever stayed long. As soon as they were making money families left to make room for the next shipful of migrants. We were given beds downstairs with the older boys and men. Women and children slept upstairs.

On my second day, a kindly Welfare Society worker drove me to meet my guardians, Norman and Nessa Kayser. Two more giving, selfless and caring people an orphan could not hope to find. Norman and Nessa were first cousins who'd fallen in love and married, devoting their lives to their three children, and their time to serving the community. Norman didn't attend synagogue any more than Nessa kept a kosher home, yet their lives were as spiritual and good as any I'd known. Norman was president of the Toorak Road synagogue and a board member of the Jewish Welfare Society. Though he lived modestly in a rented three-bedroom brick-veneer home, he gave generously of his time and intellect. His company was energising, his work for the community inspiring. Watching Norman was like seeing Tatte in action again. He made me want to be a better man.

My first encounter with the Kaysers was profoundly disappointing for Nessa. She'd spent the whole week shopping, chopping, baking and frying to create the perfect Friday-night meal, one that said 'Welcome. We want you to feel at home.' It was also a meal in need of a hungry guest, and I knew at least two helpings of each course would be required to avoid offending the doting hostess. Under normal circumstances I could have cleared the table, but that night I was fit to burst before I even sat down. Marty, the local milk-bar proprietor and self-proclaimed expert on all things Australian, had given me a tip: 'Australians don't serve large meals. At best you'll get a plate of bangers and mash, at worst some cold sangas.'

I had no idea what bangers and sangas were, but didn't want to sound more stupid than I already felt, so I took Marty's advice and bought a tin of spaghetti and a block of Cadbury's fruit-and-nut chocolate, and polished off the lot before I knocked on the Kaysers' door.

Nessa wasn't cross; she probably assumed I was a small eater. When I met with them a second time and helped myself to a fourth helping, she started to ask questions. Hadn't I liked last week's herring? Had the schnitzel been too dry? The pudding runny? I assured Nessa it had just been a case of bad culinary advice, and swore that I'd never again eat past one o'clock on a Friday. I crossed my legs as I spoke, discarding Marty's other precious piece of advice—never cross your legs while seated. According to Marty this offended Australians by reminding them of their convict roots.

I'd arrived in Melbourne with £25 in savings and a place to stay, so I didn't come to the Kaysers looking for a handout. I was looking for family, for a base from which I could explore and grow, somewhere I could go on Friday nights and birthdays. The Kayser children, Max, Lynne and Sue, looked on me as an older brother, and competed viciously for my attention and affection. Nessa always apologised for them, but she needn't have. I looked forward to the backyard footy, fancy-dress parades, piggyback rides and wrestling matches as much as the family meals that followed the madness.

I was only twenty, but I was ready for Norman's life, for the mortgage and the kids, the predictability and the security. I no longer had parents, so the next best thing was to become one. Step one towards becoming a family man was finding a job. Romance was permissible without money, but love and marriage—that could only come once I was financially secure.

Friday: The New Australian

There were two advertisements for jewellers in *The Age* newspaper that week and I headed to the city, to Forster Jewellers, the larger of the ads, on Tuesday. I sat for a short interview with the factory foreman, Len 'Squeezie' Taylor, and ten minutes later was seated opposite the big boss himself, who offered me the job. My wages would be £7 a week, Mr Forster announced, and I was to start the following Monday. That left me jobless for four days. Now that work had become a reality for me I was not keen to put it off. I headed to the second firm that had advertised, owned by a Max Hurwitz, a German immigrant in his forties. The interview went well and I was told that if I had the appropriate skills, the job was mine.

'Copy this ring. If I can't tell the difference between your work and ours, you've got the job,' Mr Hurwitz promised, and then, draping his arm over my shoulder said, 'Emil, you get this job and I'll look after you like my own son. You'll learn things here you never imagined possible.'

Two hours later, using the tools I had brought from Kosice, I handed the foreman a white-gold, delicately shouldered claw-set ring. He took it from me and, holding it up to the light in his tweezers, tilted it this way and that. He rubbed his fingers over the claws and, picking up the original Hurwitz design, cleared his throat.

'These rings aren't of the same quality. I could tell them apart immediately,' he turned to the boss. 'Emil's is by far the better made of the two.'

I didn't go home that day. I made three more rings just like the first, and waved Mr Hurwitz goodbye at six o'clock, so touched by his welcome that I failed to discuss the small matter of my wages.

I was first at my bench on Wednesday, thrilled to be working with my hands again, putting into practice all I had learnt as an apprentice in Kosice. As I rolled out one bar of gold after another, I imagined all the wonderful things Max would teach me. I envisioned spending days at my bench sculpting the perfect brooch, cutting into the gold with my diamond-tipped saw to fashion roses and bows. I imagined the diamond setters marvelling at my workmanship as they dropped opals and pear-shaped diamonds into my coronets. I pictured Melbourne's society women queuing for my pieces.

On Friday Mr Hurwitz announced my income was to be £5 10s a week.

'I'm offering you this princely sum because I think of you as a son. You've had a tough time. You deserve a little extra!'

My mouth fell open. Unfortunately, Max misread my surprise as gratitude. The reality was, I couldn't afford to live on that wage: soon I would have to leave the Welfare home and pay board—£5 was the going rate for a room. Then there was the train ticket to the city and income tax to pay. If I took Max's job over the Forster's £7 pay, I wouldn't save a cent.

'You understand, then, why I have to say no to your offer,' I concluded after running through the sums with him. But Max didn't and, red-faced and raging, he threw my pay packet at me.

'Pack your tools and get out,' he thundered, adding under his breath, 'and to think I was willing to treat you like a son.'

I turned up for work at Forster's on Monday morning. Len showed me to a bench.

'G'day. Me name's Bill. Billy Tricky. And yours?' said the

young man to my right. His smile was set off by a smart shirt, striped tie and suspenders.

'My name's Emil,' I said, taking his hand.

'And that's Jim,' he said, pointing to a tall, clean-shaven fellow hunched over the bench on my left.

'He's been in the war too. New Guinea.'

'Morning smoko's at ten, drinks at five-fifteen at the London Hotel,' Jim offered without looking up. Forty other tradesmen had their heads down.

I pulled out my tools and got to work.

What should have felt like a production line was in fact a warm, supportive workplace. The men at Forster's made quality jewellery and were secure enough in their employment to share their knowledge with a new Australian. The men didn't find my accent jarring or my small-town ways bumbling; instead, I was someone to be looked after.

Jim Cross introduced me to Australian beer and bought me my first pot. His wife introduced me to lamingtons and passionfruit sponge. Billy Tricky taught me to play 'real football'.

I started putting in overtime. I could feel my dream, conceived on the train ride to Naples, becoming a reality.

Fifteen

SEPTEMBER 2002

When I was twelve I went on a school excursion to Kew Cottages. I didn't leave my teacher's side during our two-hour stay.

'This may be the first time some of you have spoken to a disabled person. Take this opportunity to make new friends. You'll find the children here love company,' our teacher said. 'Take them outside to play or read a story together.'

It was the first time I'd seen a Down Syndrome child and I was scared—of the drool, of the wide-eyed curiosity, of not knowing what they'd do next.

When I was sixteen my grandfather became ill, too ill to care for at home. I visited him at the nursing home, daily at first, when he could still hold a conversation, and his bowels. But he got worse, and I grew frightened. Frightened of the hospital smell and the way his mind wandered. Frightened

September 2002

of the ranting from the adjacent room and the little old lady lying on the bed down the hall who never seemed to move.

I spent my twenty-first birthday in New York shopping, clubbing, visiting galleries and trying to ignore the homeless people begging for handouts under the double-glazed windows of my swank Upper West Side apartment. I used the subway but avoided the tunnels between 10.00 a.m. and 3.00 p.m. because that's when the crazies got on. I ignored half the city because I didn't understand it.

My daughter Tanya is three. She knows she has two grandfathers. My husband's father, Pa, picks her up after she's fallen over and scratched her knee on the asphalt. He scoops rainbow ice-cream into cones, plays soccer with her and carries her half-asleep to mummy's car at the end of play dates. Her other grandfather, Papa, has a chair-lift in his house that he lets her drive up and down the stairs every Thursday. He likes it when she holds his hand and climbs onto his bed to kiss his forehead. She has to be gentle with him and careful with his tubes. He can't talk to her, but if she stands in front of him, he can watch her dance. He needs help going to the toilet like she does, and sometimes her grandmother wipes his mouth, just like mummy wipes hers, after a meal. Papa's food is runny and it goes straight into his stomach through a long, clear tube. Sometimes she gets to crush his medicines and mix them with water so her grandma can pour them down his tube. Papa can't say thank you, but she knows she's done a good job because his mouth twists into a smile.

She's learnt all this and she hasn't even started school.

'Can I have it?'

'No, me!'

My children are fighting over a spider tattoo wrapped in plastic, stuck to the top of a tub of yoghurt I've pulled from the fridge.

Josh is seven and Tanya four. Tattoos are cool, and when you've tired of them, or the edges have begun to peel, you can wash them off.

My father's tattoo was permanent. I thought it lovely, the intricate leaves and delicately drawn petals, but at the same time disconcerting. Tattoos were for tough guys, mean guys who beat people up. I knew this from TV.

'Why do you have one?' I asked my father when I was eight.

'Well, I had a tattoo underneath, which wasn't pretty, so I designed this one to go over the top of it.'

'I like it,' I said, skipping to my desk to design my own. I had my father's artwork for inspiration, scraps of paper I snuck from his desk or retrieved from the bin. Jewellery designs he had doodled on bits of paper or a picture pulled from a trade magazine. Peacock brooches with sapphire plumes and sculpted bangles of corded gold; platinum wedding bands strewn with diamonds and two-tone engagement rings set off with emeralds.

September 2002

I never thought about that first tattoo, the one underneath the flower.

❦

'If I had my time over and got to choose my own ending? I'd choose this one, this disease, with all its lessons and revelations. I'd choose the "me" I've become.'

I have endless questions for my father and he answers them all, slowly tapping away at his computer, his words pulsing from the screen. Sometimes he answers questions I haven't yet thought to ask. His dying has allowed us that small compensation. The daring to ask and the courage to answer.

I have kept every print-out he has given me, and saved each email. The floppy discs on my desk contain the most intense and revealing dialogue I have ever had with my father. He has taught me how to live without uttering a single word.

Sixteen

SATURDAY: BIG BUSINESS

I wasn't aiming for a huge income, I just wanted enough money to buy my own future, to no longer be reliant upon government, charitable bodies and sponsors for my survival. I wanted to stand on my own two feet, so, two weeks after arriving in Melbourne, I convinced Eugene to move out of the Jewish Welfare home with me. We found accommodation with the Kleins, in the five-room Victorian home they shared with their daughters, Ruth and Vera. It was my first taste of family life and, when the time came, I was loathe to leave it. The Kleins' Brunswick home was always filled with conversation and noise: the sound of the milkman collecting his money and swapping full bottles of milk for empty ones; Ruth, shy behind wire-rimmed glasses, practising scales on the piano; the baker's horse dragging square loaves of white bread between houses; the whirr of the ice-box; the gurgling of the outdoor toilet; the laughter of children.

But the house was too small and Mrs Klein's sister,

Rozsi Gregus, had a bigger boarding house, an Edwardian home hidden behind a mass of hydrangeas in Stanley Street, Elsternwick, so we moved there. The Greguses' house was dark with heavy oak furniture, navy blue tie-back nylon curtains and mottled cream wallpaper. A tidy house, a showpiece, a home barely lived in. The small back garden boasted a new Hills hoist only Mrs Gregus was permitted to touch. The vinyl lounge was covered in plastic, every inch of polished wood hidden under doilies. Vases of cut crystal held artificial flowers, and porcelain ballerinas sat on display for guests who never came. Louis and Andrew moved from Armadale to join Eugene, me and two other migrant boys, George and Peter, and we spent our time cramped around a rectangular red Laminex table in the kitchen, feeding each other Jatz crackers smothered in Vegemite, wincing at the taste. We bought peanut butter and crisps, banana custard and chocolate crackles and tried them all, voting unanimously for the superiority of the European dessert—the honey cake, poppyseed cake and sour cherry slice. We listened to the big bands play dancehall favourites on the Greguses' AWA Radiola and talked about the girls we'd met over hands of gin-rummy.

The Greguses were not a happy family and I suspect Rozsi would have let us stay for free merely for the pleasure of our company and the sense of camaraderie we brought into her otherwise sterile, silent home. The Greguses had lost two daughters to the Holocaust, leaving them emptied of love for their third. They had thought that by sending their daughters to relatives in Hungary the girls would be safe from Hitler. Instead the parents were spared in Slovakia and the girls were rooted from their hideout and sent to Auschwitz. Rozsi had given her husband Sandor a third daughter, but giving was not the same as forgiving, and Mary Gregus's parents never forgave themselves or each other for letting their other daughters die.

Mary seemed to understand that her mother was too tired to play and her father too sad to smile, so she did her best to keep out of their way. So did we, and instead of discussing the unhappiness that hung in the air, rather than acknowledge that the girl's father was consumed by the twisted path his life had taken and that her mother was fixated on the love she had lost—that of her dead daughters and the husband who shared her bed but not her heart—we raised our voices in laughter. We drowned out the silence with jokes and games and friendship. It tore at me to see Mary so alone, talking to her dolls and pouring tea for imaginary friends, so I did what I could and played with her.

On my weekends off from the tea-parties, hopscotch and hide-and-seek, I made my own friends. I longed for the comfort of friends who understood my past, kids who, at eighteen, had already lived a lifetime. Kids like me who had nothing, but wanted it all. I didn't think about the camps or what might have been had my parents been spared. I refused to apportion blame or indulge in self-pity. The past was over and done with, and I wanted to surround myself with people for whom the future was bright.

I opened a bank account with the State Savings Bank of Victoria and emptied it two weeks later when I bought a rusted second-hand bicycle for £5. The clunking black-and-red bike took me through Elsternwick to Elwood's sparkling foreshore to join the swarm of Hungarian and Czech Jews picnicking on the sand, drinking cheap Australian wine from plastic cups. I'd find Louis chatting up a girl in a bikini; Andrew sprawled on a towel, his nose in a book; or Eugene slathering his pale skin with zinc cream, and I'd settle in next to them. We'd share an ice-cream and chase seagulls and pull beach balls from the salty water, glad to be on this side of the expansive blue sea.

Sundays were quieter. It took some getting used to, the city shutting down for the day: no newspapers, no cinema, no shops. Just the local milk bar open. We'd stay in bed late and listen to the radio. Later, I learnt to play tennis and canasta. Louis drove us everywhere. But soon there were too many friends to squeeze into the one battered car, so I learnt to drive. Louis taught me, on a weekend rental I split with Eugene and George. I hadn't spare change for professional tuition, so I sat the driving test having only driven circles around the local supermarket carpark.

'Well, you obviously can't drive. Tell me, mate, did you even bother to study the road laws?' the policeman asked after stopping the test short.

'I tell you what,' he continued in a whisper, 'instead of paying your £20 to a driving instructor, which is what you shoulda done in the first place, just pay me the twenty, and I'll pass you right now. Save everyone a lotta trouble.'

I bought my first car six months later but the Austin A40 didn't make it onto a main road for three months. Not till Louis had taken me back to the carpark to practise my reversing, parking and three-point turns and not till I knew the answers to every question in the road manual.

My first road trip in the Austin A40 was to Sydney during Easter. I couldn't believe my luck when Len told me I had four weeks' paid annual leave and public holidays off. I'd only got Saturdays off when I had worked as an apprentice in Kosice because my boss had been a religious Jew. I'd worked six days a week for three years with three days off in all that time. In Australia I got Saturdays *and* Sundays off, and it was never too long before a public holiday rolled by. Usually I took the time away from Forster's to work longer hours at a second job in a hotel; but that Easter, with my shiny new car, and Louis, Eugene and George egging me on, I decided to take a break.

We drove for sixteen hours straight, taking turns at the wheel. Our shipmate Philip Spiegel had relocated to Sydney and settled in King's Cross, so we started our weekend at Darlinghurst Road. Walking the Cross, I was amazed at the gall of the men calling me to sample their girls. It became a game in the end—to see how low we could bargain down the half-hour fee before changing our minds and walking on. And the shows! I'd never imagined that in hotels and bars, men and woman paid to see other couples make out. I'd never thought about sex as other than something men and women did in the privacy of their own bedrooms.

By the time I was twenty-one I had more friends than I could squeeze into my battered black address book, but I didn't have a girlfriend. I'd dated girls, taken them to dinner, to dances, introduced them to friends, made love to them in the back seat of my car, but I hadn't been in love. To meet girls I frequented town hall dances. I navigated my way from Heidelberg to Richmond, Collingwood to St Kilda, to meet pretty girls. 'Jack Trevorrow and his Modern-Airs' or 'Mil

Saturday: Big Business

Gorway and his Old Timers' would be on stage crooning and we'd walk into the hall, one more group of boys dressed in four-guinea blue twill double-breasted suits. My hair would be slick with Brylcreem, my leather shoes polished to within an inch of their life. We'd stand in clumps and survey the room: the pretty girls in full skirts cinched at the waist already dancing, their homelier friends parked on chairs, waiting to be asked. Louis had taught me the foxtrot, so I waited for the tangos and waltzes and sambas to be over. Then, as soon as the band announced a foxtrot I'd be out on the floor, circling with the other men. On a good night I'd approach a girl and, if her dance card wasn't full, she might agree to pencil me in. If the attraction was mutual, she'd slip the dance card in her pocket and we'd spend the rest of the night together. On quiet nights I'd ask the plain girls to dance so I could meet their friends.

Eventually I met Sandra, a dark-haired, doe-eyed student. She should have been 'the one'. Stimulating, supportive and smart, Sandra's insight, intelligence and wit proved every bit as powerful a turn-on as her shapely hips. I wanted to be in love, so I stuck in there for twelve months, wanting to fall hard, waiting for a spark.

My friends liked her. Berti liked her. Berti Burger, my St Gilgen pal who departed for Australia in 1949 without a forwarding address, was now back in my life. After a stint in Sydney, Berti had settled in Adelaide, set up business as a motor mechanic, and, on a weekend with mates in Melbourne, met and later proposed to Mary Haar, a seventeen-year-old Czech girl with a history much like his own. Scanning the newspaper one Sunday, an engagement notice caught my attention: 'Berti Burger to wed Mary Haar'. I grabbed the telephone directory from Sandor's desk, thumbed the pages until I found 'H', then 'Haar' and dialled the number.

Mary answered the phone. 'Yes, the Berti Burger I'm marrying *is* Romanian', and 'Yes, he did live briefly in Austria, at St Gilgen' and finally, 'Yes, he has mentioned the name Emil before.'

Mary asked, 'You're Emil Braun?'

'Yes,' I laughed, 'and I have a great idea for an engagement present.'

I surprised Berti at his engagement party six days later. He was surrounded by a throng of guests, entertaining them with the story of how he and his bride-to-be had met.

'It took just three dates and she said yes. She was dying to marry me …' the same twinkle in his eye, cheeky as ever. Then he saw me, and we ran at each other and embraced.

'Watch this guy,' Berti said, spinning me around to face his friends. 'He lies about his age.'

❦

Though Australia was undoubtedly my 'lucky country', and I was the luckier for having been accepted as a resident, there were tough times. In 1952 a serious economic recession hit, forcing Forster's management to halve the firm's labour force. To my surprise, I survived the culling while many of my workmates, some of them long-standing employees, were let go. Though I'd always been treated respectfully by the boss, I'd expected to go first, being both an immigrant and a Jew. It was hard to believe that my being Jewish didn't matter, that it no longer counted against me.

I headed to the Topsy to think. Midweek, our local diner was quiet. When the boys and I usually took over one of its twelve tables on a Saturday night, the diner was packed with Hungarian and Slovak Jews tearing at bread, shouting advice, devouring cheap schnitzel, stuffed cabbage and paprika chicken. Tucked into a dim corner of one of the city's dead-end lanes, the Topsy was our regular haunt—it and Grunfeld's Home Cooking.

I pulled up a plastic chair, ordered a bowl of chicken soup, and considered my position. I hadn't finished school, attended university or worked at other jobs. What would I do if I were let go? I needed a fallback plan, something I could do if the jewellery trade didn't work out. I listed my strengths on a paper napkin:

1. hard worker
2. needs money
3. team player

Then I wiped the remnants of dinner from my mouth, screwed up the napkin, and spent the remainder of my evening watching Laszlo, the waiter at the Topsy, attend to patrons. Why not wait tables like Laszlo, I thought. After all, how hard could it be to slop a bit of goulash on a plate? Laszlo did it, a boy of seventeen, a Holocaust orphan without schooling or experience, a boy still able to smile, a kid like me, hungry for a better life. Laszlo worked every shift he could get. He planned to have his own restaurant one day.

'It will be one of a kind,' he told us, 'a place where you can order Hungarian meatballs or an Aussie meat pie. Australian–Hungarian cuisine.'

Everyone had their dream.

Naïvely, I applied for work at the five-star Windsor Hotel. The girl at reception, mistaking my bravado for experience, slotted me in for a two o'clock interview with the banquet-room manager, Mr Goninon, a man who appeared by his girth to sample the food as often as he served it.

He ushered me in. 'I'm a busy man, so let's get straight to it. Can you "spoon and fork"?'

'Of course,' I answered, making a mental note to find out what the term meant.

Once the first lie was out, the rest was easy. 'One can't run a banquet room without such knowledge. My most recent management role was at the famed Hotel Kurtz in Prague. You've heard of it?' I ventured, hoping Goninon hadn't been to the Czech capital lately.

'Yes, of course,' Goninon answered, a little flushed. 'Who hasn't?'

I headed straight to the Topsy for Laszlo's advice. Though Laszlo didn't spoon and fork he knew all about fine dining. In a classy hotel like the Windsor, he instructed, the waiters placed empty, hot plates in front of guests. Food was brought from the kitchen on silver platters, and each guest was served with a spoon and fork.

'Come, I'll show you,' Laszlo offered, throwing open the doors to the kitchen.

I walked through the double doors of the Windsor Hotel the next day at five minutes to six after ducking into the hotel's toilet to change from my work clothes into a hired white shirt, bow tie and black pants. Goninon directed me to a corner of the banquet room with instructions to set three tables, seat the guests, and serve dinner. Laszlo's instructions had been limited to a demonstration of the 'spoon and fork'. I hadn't thought to practise, or to ask how to set a table or pour the wine. So I got busy polishing a fork, all the while watching the fellow next to me lay his table. I studied him gliding to the right of a guest to pour a drink, then approach from the left to spoon and fork. Then I did the same.

'Imagine having to hire a formal suit every time you go out to eat,' I whispered to another waiter as we exited the kitchen.

'Don't be daft,' he said. 'The people who dine here own their suits, and they probably have more than one. No point dwelling on it. You'll never have money like that.'

But I will, I said to myself. Just you wait and see.

I sat down to eat at a tableful of waiters as the last guest departed the room. The leftovers were cold, but tasted every bit as good as I'd imagined. I gorged myself on rack of lamb, sautéed beans, squash and mashed potatoes and was just about to launch into a Bombe Alaska when Goninon summoned me. I managed a mouthful of dessert and followed him to his office.

'So, you know how to spoon and fork, do you?' Goninon smirked. 'And I'm the Prince of Egypt.'

My boss's voice grew tremulous.

'You lying bastard,' he began. Goninon knew lots of dirty words, and in the space of five minutes used them all. Exhausted from the effort of stringing together so many expletives, he eventually fell silent. I took a step back, expecting fists where his mouth had left off, but we didn't come to blows. Instead, Goninon sat down, wiped his glistening forehead with his shirt sleeve and smiled.

'I like you, Emil Braun. You've got guts. Report for work tomorrow at six.'

The dream home I'd been saving for seemed a distant reality. To speed things along I took a third job, waiting tables at the more illustrious Hotel Menzies. From 8.00 a.m. to 5.00 p.m. I sculpted silver and gold to hold diamonds, opals, gems and precious stones. At night I seated the wealthy guests who wore my work—turquoise brooches bought to match umbrella handles, pill boxes and powder compacts; bracelets of plaited gold; cascading diamond pendants; burnished gold bangles. I poured French champagne for prime minister Menzies and offered petits fours to Sir Dallas Brooks, before catching the train home to my £5-a-week boarding house.

Reluctantly, after three years at Forster's I gave notice; I needed more money. I settled for a job paying £2 a week more, around the corner at Harry 'Moniek' Granek's. The fact that there were only three of us on the benches meant I was able to do more varied work and have direct contact with customers and suppliers. It was an invaluable experience for a business rookie, and boosted my knowledge of the trade—and my English. I began to plan my future as head of my own jewellery empire.

I knew that, with time, people would come to know my work and trust me, that my name would stand for something. That people would hand over their diamonds and place orders for my intricate, innovative designs. I produced delicate pieces: bird-of-paradise brooches, ballerina clips, rings of finely corded gold, filigreed platinum wedding bands spangled with brilliants. The war was over and with it went drabness and austerity. Women aspired to be elegant and feminine again and wanted jewellery to match.

But I was impatient, I wanted the empire now. I wanted to be a boss. I'd been controlled for so long: by my father, the Nazis, camp commanders and employers. I was desperate, so when Louis mentioned he'd seen a delicatessen for sale and suggested we buy it in partnership, I jumped at the chance, ignoring the fact that I knew nothing about leasing, contracts or how to slice rye bread. After all, what credentials did you need to sell ham and cheese on rye?

Apparently all you needed was money — or so the ad read for the 'Deli ... going cheap'. £6750, to be exact. We had only £1500 between us. We looked at the figures, sampled the food, counted the customers, scanned the shelves and finally put the hard word on the agent. If we were going deep into debt we wanted some assurances about the lease and the profits. The agent ('Hey, I'm a friend, call me Don'), a tanned middle-aged bachelor with manicured hands and a smooth tongue, took my hand and, shaking it warmly, congratulated me on possessing a wisdom beyond my years.

'You're two smart men. I can see that nothing gets past you two. Born businessmen, you are.'

His smile widened.

'The lease is fine. It expires in six months, but after that, it's up to you. Extend it as long as you like. And as for the profits, I'll tell you what, the vendor will throw in a two-week trial period. That way you get to see the money coming in before you sign up. Deal?'

'What a guy,' we thought as we entered his agency two weeks later to sign contracts. I handed over the £300 deposit and pocketed one copy of the Sale of Business contract, barely scanning the legal jargon scrawled across its four pages. Don was right—all that fine print was just the lawyers' way of making a buck. We all knew the deal, and going on the last two weeks' profits, the deal was good.

We could hardly wait to share the good news with our friends.

'We're businessmen!' we laughed. 'This must be a record. We've only been in Australia three years.'

'So, you're businessmen?' Norman Kayser asked. 'Then I suppose you'll need a lawyer. You know, to transfer the business to your name, to make everything kosher.'

We went to see Norman's solicitor the next day. Newton Super, a short, fleshy man with a sympathetic face, ushered us into his office, and disappeared behind a large oak desk covered with files, to which he added our contract. As he perused the document, I surveyed the room. The floor was littered with discarded memoranda, briefs and dog-eared legal journals, the walls cluttered with an impressive array of university degrees and honorary certificates. The room was a mess; I hoped the lawyer's mind was a little clearer.

Mr Super looked up. He wasn't smiling.

'Just one question, boys. Why didn't you show me the contract before signing it?'

I suddenly knew we had made a terrible mistake. Mr Super

made just one phone call—to the property owner—and he asked one question: what were his intentions regarding the lease? The landlord's intention at the end of the six-month lease, Mr Super told us as he hung up the phone, was to take possession of the shop himself. No further lease would be granted. And yes, the vendor's agent had been told, months ago.

'I'm sorry,' Mr Super offered. 'I can see by your expressions that you both understand what has just happened.'

We understood. We'd just paid £6750 for nothing and, according to our lawyer, there was nothing we could do about it. We'd paid our deposit, signed a contract and would have to come up with the balance of the purchase price in thirty days.

I left Mr Super's office, forcing back tears, Louis miserable beside me. The prospect of working the next ten years to rectify our mistake was only made worse by the realisation that the agent had probably already banked his commission. I hadn't felt hatred for a long time, but now it propelled me forward and around the block to the real estate agency. It was after five, but Don was still in, working a young couple up a few thousand dollars to purchase their dream home.

'Don, g'day,' I said in the cheeriest tone I could muster. 'We don't mean to butt in, but could you just pass us your copy of the deli contract? We've left ours at home and I just wanted to check something before paying the balance of the purchase price.'

Don rushed at his filing cabinet, dollar signs illuminating the way.

He slapped the only remaining evidence of our stupidity

on the counter in front of us, and returned to the business of ripping off another young couple. I opened the contract and stared at it, but all I could see was the word 'sucker' repeating itself across the page.

'Louis,' I whispered, 'we're not working for the next ten years to buy this arsehole a new car. Here,' I said, shoving the contract deep into his jacket pocket, 'take this and run. Run to the darkest alley you can find and tear the thing to shreds. I'll stay with Don and hold him back if I have to.'

'Where's he off to then?' Don demanded, realising his only copy of the contract had left the office with Louis.

'To the toilet. He was busting,' I answered.

'With the contract?' Don's voice was loud, edgy. The young couple shifted uneasily in their seats.

'I guess he needed something to wipe himself with,' I offered.

The expected stream of abuse followed, with Don threatening bodily harm, endless litigation and a call to the cops. Sadly, his star witnesses, the young couple standing not two feet away from Louis at the time, denied seeing a young man with a contract leaving the shop and promptly left the premises themselves. I sat there, unmoved by all the commotion.

'Call the police, then. I'll wait. They may be interested in what I have to say about your so-called legal document,' I suggested.

Meanwhile, blocks away in a derelict alley, Louis sat on the dirty ground, ripping Don's document into tiny pieces.

I waited for one hour—for the police, for Don to calm down, for Louis to set us free. I got tired of waiting. Don was

Saturday: Big Business

clearly bluffing and I was growing tired of his game; it had become boring. Besides, I was hungry.

'If you're not serving dinner, Don, I'm afraid I'm going to have to leave,' I said.

'And I'll see to it that you're both thrown in jail,' Don replied weakly.

I extended my hand and wished Don good luck, thanking him for all he had taught me.

We saw Mr Super the next day, accepting his assessment of our behaviour as 'criminal' and his congratulations on a job well done. A month later we saw him again. This time he handed us a cheque for £300, our deposit. I was too stunned to ask how he'd gotten the money back, but extremely grateful, especially when he showed us the door without giving us a bill.

'This one's on me, boys. Next time, I'll charge. And next time, come and see me before you sign anything.'

❦

By 1955 the deli fiasco was sufficiently dulled in my memory to allow for a renewed interest in business. Louis had risked a secure income as a motor mechanic to try his hand with his brother Andrew in a city sandwich bar, and I, too, felt ready to go it alone. I'd worked in the jewellery trade for some time, was older and wiser, and had a good lawyer. I told Mr Granek of my plans to go out on my own, giving what I felt was a generous notice period.

'It's just something I'm thinking about,' I told him. 'Of course, I'll stay for as long as you like. One month, two …'

He cut me off. 'You're fired.'

I cleared out my belongings and squeezed a second-hand bench into my bedroom. I worked on engagement-ring samples, leaving holes where the diamonds would be. I designed business cards and practised sales pitches. When I had fourteen diamond-ring mounts I hit the streets looking for a city address. I secured a bench in a tiny workshop at 288 Little Collins Street, trading £2 10s a week in rent for business credibility. I visited every wholesaler and retailer in Melbourne, and was politely rejected by every one of them. Still, they answered the door when I knocked, so I kept knocking, paying them return visits each week, sometimes twice a week.

Mr Thurin, the owner of Rundles, a large city store on the corner of Elizabeth and Little Collins Street, was the first jeweller I wore down.

'I respect a fighter,' Thurin grinned, opening his office door, 'but I don't need any rings, and won't buy any. Still, your efforts deserve the courtesy of a showing. So, what do you have there, Emil?'

I opened a black leather, velvet-lined box containing twenty-four gold ring mounts. I knew other manufacturers showed three, maybe four at a time. Choice was not their strong point. Thurin's grin stretched into a smile. He plucked a design from the velvet case, ran his fingers over it and held it up to the light.

'Smooth,' he said. 'Nice work front and back.'

One hour later Thurin was still smiling. 'I'll have five dozen of the claw-set filigree design, by the end of the month, if you can manage it.'

Saturday: Big Business

Of course I could manage it. The fact that I wouldn't see daylight for three weeks, that I'd have to work, sleep and eat at my bench, escaping my bedroom at night only to wait tables, was immaterial. I had a customer. And a big order to fill.

Once I'd made the rings and delivered them to the diamond setter, I was back on the road, trying to get more orders. Mr Moore, of W.J. Moore & Sons, who had turned me away more than a dozen times, opened the door to his factory.

'Tell me, Emil,' he said, 'have you even sold a single ring?'

'Well, yes,' I answered. 'In fact I've just come from dropping off five dozen at Rundles.'

Mr Moore knew Thurin was finicky, the finickiest man in the business. If Thurin had seen something in my designs, Moore figured, there was probably something worth looking at.

Mr Moore let me in. I left one hour later with my second order.

On the strength of those orders, I secured a third order for fifty ring mounts from another jeweller. Mr Algendas wanted to set my mounts with diamonds bought from a Mr Fajnkind and promised to pay within thirty days. I delivered the mounts and was still waiting for my cheque six months later. I'd telephoned and sent letters; now I was at his door. People always liked the personal touch.

'Mr Algendas, I'm here for my money,' I stepped into the dusty showroom. 'I did call. Your secretary obviously doesn't pass on messages.'

'Ah, Emil, I'm so sorry,' Algendas explained. 'I instructed the accountant to write your cheque out weeks ago. I'm sure it's in the mail.'

I wasn't familiar with the expression 'the cheque is in the mail', but I did know small-time businessmen didn't have accountants write their cheques. His under-used chequebook was probably in the desk drawer beside him.

'I'm afraid I've been burnt before, Mr Algendas, and it's made me a little cynical. Would you mind very much, just to put me at ease, bringing out the rings so I could see them?'

Algendas had no choice. He slunk off to his safe and returned with a case of seventy-two rings. My fifty were there as well as twenty-two others, all set with Fajnkind's diamonds. I painstakingly inspected each one, figuring Algendas would grow restless and return to some other, more profitable task. He did, and as soon as his back was turned I grabbed the case of rings and shot out the door. I didn't take the lift. I ran down the stairs, straight to Fajnkind's office.

'Louis will love this story,' I thought, while explaining the day's events to Fajnkind. We agreed over a beer that I'd remove his diamonds from my rings and return the diamonds to him, together with the twenty-two spare rings, for him to do as he pleased.

Algendas was not so pleased. 'You're a thief and a scoundrel, Emil Braun, and I'll see to it you end up in jail!' he yelled over the phone.

'Why so upset, Mr Algendas?' I teased. 'The ring mounts are still here, unset, of course, and the diamonds are with Mr Fajnkind. I'll hold the rings for you for two weeks, and when you pay me, they'll be yours. If you'd rather file a police report, however, be my guest.'

Algendas never filed a police complaint. Nor did he pay for the rings. He went broke.

Business boomed, and not a minute too soon. I'd been knocking on doors for six months before I secured the Thurin order, and the constant rejections and my depleted bank account were starting to wear away at my confidence. I had begun to doubt myself.

Six months later I had the key to a new office. I'd outgrown my Little Collins Street sublet and now worked day and night in York House alongside seventy other businesses. Diamond merchants, setters, pearl threaders and metallurgists shared the twelve-storey Art Deco city tower otherwise known as the 'jewellery heart of Melbourne'. At £750 key money, the five-square-metre room was considered a steal, despite the fact it hadn't been cleaned for a decade and needed repainting.

I was forced to give up waiting tables. It was either that or get no sleep at all. I was working eighteen-hour days and visiting the bank to deposit cheques more often than I was visiting friends. One morning, as I was making coffee for myself, I stopped to pore over my bank statement. Usually I went straight to the balance. If it was positive, I moved on to the newspaper. That day I didn't get to the paper. The figure at the foot of the page was more positive than I'd ever seen it. It was enough to earn interest! Enough, I realised, to pay a wage.

That night I celebrated with Louis, and then a fortnight later again, with Don Marshall, my first employee.

Seventeen

FEBRUARY 2002

I grew up doing all the things my parents never got to do: ballet class, tennis lessons, skiing, piano. My inability to stand on pointes, a weak backhand and the fact I was tone-deaf didn't alter my parents' resolve.

'Talent is not the point,' my father would preach, nudging me out the door to ballet class. 'Brauns don't quit and we definitely don't take the easy way out.'

Go for it, was how my father lived his life, how we were made to live ours. If we failed at a task we tried again. If we lacked a skill, we practised until we developed it. We were taught to succeed, to relish a challenge. So I practised my scales and skiied through blizzards until a time came when I looked around and found myself doing these things because I wanted to. My father had withdrawn the bribes that he'd used to tempt me into so many lessons without my noticing.

Now, after decades of following the path of most resistance — six subjects instead of five in my final year of school; a double degree at university instead of one — I don't think I could go the easy route. My father has me convinced that with a little hard work, anything is possible.

I watch my father get up each day, get showered and dressed and fed and led and suctioned and wiped when he could stay in bed and ask for the bed pan. When he could close the curtains and still his hands and let others do his thinking. When he could say 'no' to the physiotherapy, occupational therapy and speech therapy, and 'yes' to the remote control. Refuse the potions and lotions and herbs and pills, and make the end come sooner. But that's not my father.

It's Shaun's fortieth birthday. In an effort to stave off middle-age we have invited thirty of our closest friends to join us at a sea-side resort town for a weekend of surfing, dancing and drinking. Instead of lazing by the pool mid-afternoon drinking cocktails, I have an appointment to visit a hair salon. I need to turn out a good top half because, at thirty-two weeks pregnant, the rest of me is the size of a house.

'I want my hair straight, sleek and sophisticated,' I tell the hairdresser, but she can't help the humidity and by the time I return to the hotel, curls have reformed.

I unlock the door to our hotel room and head for the hairdryer. The phone rings and I turn from the mirror to pick up. It's Mum.

'Hi, darling,' her voice is edged with sadness. She wants to be with us to celebrate Shaun's ascent into middle-age. She passes the phone to my father.

'Give Shaun a hug and have a dance for me,' Dad's electronic mouthpiece bleeps.

The phone cuts out. I don't turn the hairdryer on; I put it away and head for the lounge, to our friends.

Two weeks later it's grandparents' day at my son's school. Though my father can no longer applaud his grandson, take photos of the children parading as Noah's Ark, or thank the teachers, he insists on attending. My mother guides him from the front seat of their car to his wheelchair, gripping him tightly. They've arrived fifteen minutes early to allow for suctioning before the show. My son Josh is dressed as a lion, and comes roaring and clawing up to his Papa. His friends hang back, watching as Josh climbs aboard the wheelchair to kiss his grandfather's prickly cheek, once, twice, three times. It's a game they've played since Josh was a toddler. Now it's Papa's turn, and he brushes his lips across his grandson's cheek, neither of them admitting that one half of the 'kissing machine' isn't quite puckering up. Dad motions Mum to wheel him into the front row. It doesn't cross his mind that there he will be under the direct gaze of a hundred curious schoolchildren, or that other grandparents will have to squeeze past him to be seated.

'What other people see when they look at me doesn't concern me. What they think is unimportant. What matters is whether I make it to the concert,' my father tells me. I know he means this because I've spent days at a time with him and not once did he stop to glance in a mirror or ask that I comb his hair or straighten his jacket. It must be liberating, not caring, not seeing yourself through other people's eyes. Being who you are and not apologising for it.

February 2002

I wasn't allowed to hate my brothers. They could pull my pigtails, decapitate my Barbie dolls, refuse to take me to the movies and still I had to love them.

'Talk to your brothers,' Dad would suggest, brushing away my tears, peeling me from his neck, sending me back to the room they shared.

'Tell them I said they *have* to let you in.'

It was time for Dad to let his siblings in, to talk to them while he still could. His speech had begun to slur and his words ran together. His voice was slipping away and soon it would be difficult to be understood. And he had so much to say. Especially now.

My father had lost touch with his brother Alex and sister Cili decades ago; he'd fought so hard to build his new life in Australia that he'd lost touch with the old. Rozsi, his eldest sister, had died of cancer years ago and Alex and Cili were no more a part of his world now than Rozsi was. They lived in the old days, practising the old ways. Cili still baked her own *challah*, just like their Mamme used to, and her home felt, in so many ways, so much like Tatte's. Alex had tried to live in Australia in the sixties, but had missed the food, language and familiarity of the old country. He chose to remember a happy childhood and booked his flight back home.

Once he'd made some money, my father returned to Europe every second year on business trips, wanting to speak English and share with his siblings all the wonderful things his new life offered him. He wanted to share his prosperity, but the gifts he brought Alex and Cili—sheepskin rugs, pearl earrings, envelopes filled with American currency—never felt like enough. Or sometimes it seemed too much. He wanted to tell his brother about his daughter's skiing lessons and show him photos of the family camping trip to Central Australia where he'd dug for opals with his sons. He wanted to tell Cili about the double-storey house he was building and how smart his wife was in business. But it felt like bragging and he didn't think they'd understand. And as the years passed without letters or birthday presents he'd come to feel that the distance that had grown between them was his fault.

He wasn't sure how news of his dying would affect them. He wanted them to care, but more than that, he wanted to say goodbye. He wanted one last hug from Alex and a kiss from his sister. It was May 1998 when my father flew, with my mother, to Europe.

Cili flew from Prague to Vienna and, together with Alex, drove out to the airport to collect my parents. A table had been laid, and heaped platters of goulash, tureens of chicken soup, and trays of potato, beans and beef sat steaming alongside bottles of chilled soda water and a rectangle of poppyseed cake. An intimate lunch for four stretched into afternoon tea and then dinner. They talked late into the night, catching up, getting reacquainted, resuming a sense of family. All the years in between their shared childhood and 'now' didn't matter anymore because he was their little brother and they shared Porubka, growing up without friends, surviving the war, and losing Mamme, Tatte and Willie.

The guest list expanded, and the dining table extended, as the four became six, then eight, then more. Alex hadn't kept my father's illness a secret. Phone calls had been made and letters dispatched throughout the continent. Nieces and nephews, their husbands, wives and children surprised my parents, driving or flying to Vienna from Slovakia, the Czech Republic and as far afield as Tel Aviv.

Suddenly there seemed so much to say, and soon there would be no more talking, so my parents returned early the next day to Alex's apartment. Alex let them in, then disappeared to the kitchen to prepare a breakfast of buttered rye bread and honeyed tea. My father looked around the apartment. It looked just the same as his brother's previous home in Vienna and the same as the apartment he had lived in before that. The wallpaper in this otherwise modern, box-shaped complex was from decades past, a brown floral; the carpet equally staid. Plush soft-toys and oversized bears, a relic of Alex's son's childhood, sat gathering dust in the corners of the room. China dolls with ruby red lips and stiff blonde curls—his wife's prized collection—had not been moved from their display since Berta's death. Czech crystal vases, hand-cut bowls and glass ashtrays crowded for space in a glass cabinet next to porcelain figurines of ballerinas, circus dogs and pouting clowns. Crocheted doilies covered every inch of exposed wood.

My father had always seen his brother's resistance to change and his refusal to replace the old with the new puzzling; his need to cling to the past, unhealthy. He looked around the room, heavy with memories of his brother's dead wife, their child's infancy and the life they had lived in Czechoslovakia, and saw for the first time something of himself: a respect for life and an appreciation for all they had been given. All that Alex held dear was in this room and he didn't want to let one bit of it go. My father knew how that felt.

Alex called my parents into the kitchen. Cili arrived and they sat down to eat.

Later that day, they drove my parents to the airport. Alex left in tears. Cili kissed my father.

'Elyuka, we'll miss you,' she said, as my father disappeared behind a security barrier. My father called me from the Qantas departure lounge.

'They love me,' he told me. 'If not for this bastard of a disease, I might never have known.'

Eighteen

SUNDAY: JUDY

The magic that I'd been so desperate to find in the layback seats of my Austin A40 arrived with Judy Tarjan or, more accurately, with the black-and-white photo of her that preceded her arrival. Sandor had passed around the photo of his Hungarian niece as a means of introducing us to the eighteen-year-old who, he informed us, would be moving into the spare bedroom. He didn't mean to cast a spell over us. He had no inkling of the feelings the raven-haired beauty would arouse in his boarders. Sandor was too self-absorbed to notice the care with which each of the six men living under his roof had dressed the morning of their new housemate's arrival. He didn't hear the bickering about who should collect her from the station, or notice the lots that were drawn to determine who would act as her tour guide.

I wanted no part of my housemates' competition. I let George pick Judy up from the train station and remained silent when Peter offered to show her around the city. I planned to wait until the time was right and, when I was sure she would accept my invitation, ask Judy out. Besides, George was too desperate to impress and Peter, though sweet, was a drifter.

I suggested to Sandra that we date other people to test our feelings for each other. She agreed, on the proviso that if we did get back together, it would be forever. The wait was not easy. Judy was different from other girls I had met so far, who were either worldly, intelligent and ambitious, or demure and modest. Judy appeared to be both. I introduced myself in Hungarian. She smiled, offered her hand and asked that, whenever possible, I speak to her slowly in English. On her second day, when Peter asked if she'd like a tour of the city, she demurred, in favour of directions to the nearest bookseller. She returned an hour later, disappearing into Sandor's study, with a Hungarian–English dictionary tucked under her arm and the remnants of a newspaper—the jobs section—criss-crossed with red pen.

She waved us goodbye the following morning, her pocket dictionary still under her arm, eager to start work soldering electric cord at the Astor Radio Factory. I was waiting at the dining table when she returned that evening. Her arms were blistered, her clothes singed and her hair smelt of chemicals, but she was smiling. She sat down at the table with six boys' eyes upon her, not caring a whit about how she looked. She placed her dictionary beside her plate, picked up her spoon and ate hungrily, pausing only to look up the correct way to thank her hosts in English for a delicious dinner.

'I'm going to marry that blistered, beautiful girl,' I told myself.

Sunday: Judy

Six weeks after she arrived I asked her out. We caught a tram to St Kilda, shared a Viennese torte in Acland Street and ended the night dancing to Cliff Blundell's Wonder Band at Earl's Court. By the end of the month we were dating. It didn't matter where we went—to the Topsy for dinner, to the Esquire for a double bill, dancing at the Martini ballroom or shopping for fruit at the Queen Victoria Market; Judy seemed happy. She didn't expect lavish gifts or expensive dinners; she just wanted to talk. I found myself telling her things I'd never shared with anyone: childhood secrets, frightening dreams, fanciful plans. She listened and encouraged me to dream, not of faraway places and better times, as Mamme had, but of what I could do, here and now.

Louis was married by now. Ruth Klein, no longer shy behind wire-rimmed spectacles, had captured his heart—and Judy's. The girls were alike in many ways: both were smart, independent and warm, and they became fast friends. On warm summer evenings I'd invite the Adlers and Mary and Berti over, and call Judy from her room. We'd eat outside in the garden. Rozsi would serve potato salad and kosher chicken and a jug of hot tea and Sandor would hold his tongue because he wanted his niece married and out of his hair.

The other boys would join us if it wasn't one of Hal's super-select dance nights at the Trocadero. But Eugene would stay home, squeezing pimples in his room, hating his solitude, blaming the war. Eugene worked as a cutter in a textile business. He earned a reasonable wage and was a reasonable-looking guy, but he saw us leaving jobs, realising dreams, with girls on our arms, and he grew envious.

'Where's Eugene?' I asked Rozsi one evening, when he hadn't appeared for dinner.

'Gone,' she said. 'America, I think.'

I received a letter three months later: a wedding invitation. Eugene was marrying the daughter of a publisher. I hoped he was happy.

It took me eight weeks and twenty-two dates before I dared to hold Judy's hand. It was a warm Sunday afternoon at Mount Macedon. I offered Judy my hand, under the guise of helping her up a steep cliff, and she took it. At the top, neither of us released our grip.

Twelve months later I finally popped the question at Sandringham Beach. I half-expected her to say no, but I expected her to say something. Instead she sat there, staring in total silence at the ring I had offered her. Finally, with a mournful expression, she lifted her sweater just above her navel and explained why she couldn't be my wife.

'See this scar, Emil? This is why I can't marry you.'

A jagged scar, ten centimetres long, puckered the brown smoothness of her skin.

'It happened when I was ten years old. I can't have children. Not ever.'

I felt numb, yet at the same time incredibly clear about one thing. I did want children, but I wanted to marry Judy Tarjan more.

'It doesn't matter. I want you. There's always adoption,' I offered weakly.

It wasn't the answer she wanted. She liked me very much, she told me, but she just wasn't ready for a marriage proposal; she was too young.

Sunday: Judy

'Couldn't we wait a couple of years?' she asked.

I couldn't, so we stopped dating.

Dejected, I returned to the comfort and safety of Sandra. After each date with her, I'd make sure to give Rozsi a full report, knowing her loose lips would have Judy fully briefed by morning. I wanted to make her jealous, but it wasn't fair—to Sandra or to me—so I broke up with Sandra, this time offering no illusions about a happily-ever-after. Judy, I figured, didn't need to know about the break-up; not just yet.

Living with me and seeing me happily dating someone else wasn't easy for Judy, who was also dating but not falling in love. I lent a sympathetic ear when she complained of the lack of good, smart, strong, kind men—men who challenged her and were willing to wait to bed her. I proffered advice and lavished her with sympathy. I was charming, understanding and, as far as she knew, totally at peace with our new friendship. It drove her crazy and, eventually, back into my arms.

Six months after we resumed our relationship, we left the house by foot one evening and headed to Elwood beach. I smoothed a rug over the soft sand and we lay side by side, on our backs, looking up at the night sky, at stars different from those seen in Europe. I sat up and turned Judy's face towards me.

'Let's start our life together,' I asked.

This time she said yes.

❧

We purchased our first house at 6 McMillan Street, Elsternwick, in December 1958. I had only a few hundred pounds to my name so I borrowed the bulk of the deposit monies from Louis and the balance of the purchase price from the bank. I loved the idea of owning a piece of Australia—even if I was going to have to live there alone. It was made clear to me long ago that Judy would not be sharing my bed until after our wedding, until she was Mrs Braun. I didn't try to convince her otherwise. Though desperate to sleep with her, I found her innocence beguiling and, after a time, I became protective and proud of her resolve.

The house was a renovator's dream: paint peeling and discoloured walls; no hot water; an outside toilet; twenties kitchen; rusted corrugated-iron shower stall. I wanted it transformed by March, Judy's birthday, and our scheduled engagement party. It was Judy's idea and a stroke of genius: host a pre-engagement party at the house and call it a 'Painting Party'. We sent out invitations to forty guests. And forty guests came, armed with ammonia, rags, steel wool and paint-brushes. We supplied the ladders, paint and beer. We pulled up carpet, blasted calsomine off the walls, scrubbed rust from the showerhead, and repainted the interior in Dulux Sandstone. A week later we sent out 'Garden Party' invitations, serving wine and cheese after the weeding was done.

We furnished the house with second-hand goods from charity bins and auction houses, spending a little extra on the two single beds we bought new for Judy's parents.

'That's how couples sleep in Europe,' Judy explained, noticing my worried expression, reassuring me she considered herself a modern girl, a double-bed kind of girl.

My prospective parents-in-law arrived from Budapest on

4 July 1959, the day before our wedding. I stood under the wedding canopy at Elwood Synagogue, knees shaking, beside Edith and Ernest Tarjan, two strangers I wanted so badly to like me. Then Judy swept down the aisle and all thoughts fell away, except that I was the luckiest man on the planet.

Later that night, after a supper dance in Elwood, we fell into bed, exhausted by too many tangos and tipsy from too much red wine. Judy asked that I be careful; she didn't want to get pregnant our first time together. Sensing my bewilderment, she lifted her nightie.

'I'm not infertile; it's a burn. Boiling water. I'm sorry I deceived you. I just had to know that you were marrying me for me, not just to attain some goal you'd set for yourself — you know, a wife, three kids, a house in the suburbs. I needed to know you loved me. I know how much you wanted a family.'

'Of course I love you. It was always about us,' I stammered, and we hugged and cried, made love tentatively the first time, explosively the second, then cried some more.

I had plenty of time to find out if Judy's parents approved of me, for as soon as I'd offered our house to them, Edith was unpacking her bags and rearranging furniture.

Things started off well. Edith worked tirelessly to keep the house clean and the pantry stocked with honey cake and apricot jam. Ernest did the shopping and ran errands. They promised to help out when we had children.

I justified the loss of privacy and autonomy by telling myself that I was keeping my wife happy and giving our children the gift of live-in grandparents. I'd wished for a big family and now I had one, except sometimes it felt just a little too big. Or perhaps I felt too big to be living with parents.

Ernest was more friend than parent. A tubby, grinning man, mischievous yet shy, he was happiest making the rest of us smile. He wanted little else but to be with his family.

Edith wanted more. She wanted to be with her daughter, but she also wanted her old life back. She missed her friends, her career and her home. Though stick-thin and little taller than a ten-year-old, Edith was strong and determined, with a clear picture of what life ought to be like. She was too much like me.

Though she quickly learnt English and found full-time work as a receptionist with Telecom, Edith still missed Hungary. Her continued allegiance to the old country and preference for all things European tore at me. I was painfully patriotic and equally blinkered when it came to Australia, so we fought often and to no avail, trying to convince the other that our choice of homeland was the only sane choice. We argued about where paintings should hang and who should answer the door for guests. We argued not because we didn't like each other, but because we both thought winning would prove our dominance. Unlike me, Edith's Holocaust experience had left her lacking in self-confidence, sceptical and unsure of her place in the world. Having her own address would have helped rebuild her sense of self and allow her the self-determination we both craved.

Edith was a tireless and loyal worker, and though in hindsight we may both have been better off with separate careers, I offered her a secretarial job. Edith was a star employee. Though often tired at home she always turned on the charm for clients. She thrived in the busy city environment, forming relationships not just with the clients but with our bankers, suppliers, postal workers and the men who made our lunches at the local café. She was happiest at work and put in long hours, freeing me to pursue other interests.

After a time, Ernest worked as a photographer, capturing a world of smiles and freezing happiness on film. He attended weddings, Bar Mitzvahs and birthday parties, often uninvited but never turned away. His photos were unspectacular, but cheap and irresistible, given that they showed his clients at their most relaxed and happy. He sold enough to pay us board. Edith's wage paid for trips to Budapest and her opera and philharmonic subscriptions.

The business continued to prosper. Don Marshall was a good jeweller and a decent guy, so I paid him £3 a week more than the going rate. I liked having company at the workbench, and the money his work brought in paid for his wage and then some. Jim Cross came over from Forster's and others followed him, the word on the street being that I paid way above award rates. The way I figured it, the more experienced jewellers I secured, the better jewellery we produced and the more we sold. Emil Braun Jewellers, *'engagement rings a speciality',* moved premises five times, each time to a larger box within York House.

By 1960 I had seven men in the workshop and clients in Brisbane. I could afford to start a family. We'd only been sleeping together for three months, were still getting to know each other's bodies, when Judy took my hand and, lifting her nightie, placed my open hand on her belly.

'We're having a baby,' she whispered.

I felt her belly every night for nine months—still and flat at first, then round and fluttering with life, later swollen and stretched taut. I listened to the little Braun heartbeat, felt my child kick at his confinement. Peter was born on 26 July 1960, as angelic in those first few days of life as he was later, a toddler with clear blue eyes and blond curly locks, the child I'd imagined on the train to Naples. I gave him the Hebrew name Aaron, my father's name.

Two years later Gary was born, a round, smiling child, cheeky from the moment of his birth. We gave him the middle name William, for my brother Willie. Our third child, Suzy, was born on 9 January 1966. I cried when I saw her, and saw, in her, my mother.

Judy stayed home with the children. She was itching to get out in the real world and work.

'I'll study computers,' she said, 'or engineering or maths.'

Cooking didn't interest her or housework or knitting, but the children did, so she committed herself to them and delayed her own dreams until our youngest was in school.

We soon outgrew our home at McMillan Street. Though Peter and Gary were happy sleeping in the dining room, eating in shifts at a kitchen table that only seated four was inconvenient. I'd promised Judy when I married her that one day we'd move into a big, comfortable home in a leafy, suburban street. In 1966, with sixteen jewellers in my employ and Emil Braun Jewellers the biggest diamond-ring-mount manufacturer in Australia, I could afford to make good on that promise. We purchased a block in North Caulfield for £8500, demolished the old home on it, and commissioned an architect, Harry Ernest, to design our dream home—a double-storey, double-brick residence complete with carport, rumpus room and separate living quarters for Judy's parents.

Twelve months later we sold McMillan Street and moved into our new home, with no funds left to furnish it. We kept the cardboard boxes we'd packed our crockery in, and used them as chairs. We hung sheets for curtains and tacked the children's artwork on bare walls. We couldn't afford carpets, a lounge suite or bedside tables. Our very large house was very empty, but all ours.

Standing in the driveway of our home, the rooms bare but overflowing with the sound of children's laughter, my beautiful wife's silhouette visible through the bedroom window, I wondered if Tatte, somewhere in the heavens, could see me. Or maybe he'd been watching all along.

Nineteen

APRIL 1998

My father stops talking. It takes me some time to realise he has finished his story. What about the rest, I want to say. What about all those meetings? The hours spent fundraising? The overseas business trips? Your years on council? The property developments? The commitments and passions and absences that shaped you?

And then, sensing I expect more, want more, my father continues.

'You wanted to know who I am. Maybe I make more sense to you now, knowing about my family and the war and my work. But that's not all I am. I am "me" because of what came after. You came after, and with you three kids came my second childhood and laughter and love. Feeling your mittened fingers wrapped around my legs as I took you, knees knocking, down the snowy slopes of Mount Buller. Pushing you up and out of the cool, muddy waters of the Murray River

April 1998

and watching the speedboat drag you away on skis, your knuckles white from gripping the rope so hard. Wrapping string around your wobbly front teeth and rewarding your bravery with a visit from the tooth fairy. Sleeping in tents in the backyard and soaking bloodied knees in Dettol. Playing I-spy in the car. That's who I am. I've talked for nine nights but I can tell you who I am in less than a minute: I'm a man, loved by a beautiful woman, graced with incredible kids. A lucky man.'

I stop recording, eject the videotape from the recorder and place it deep within my handbag. My father looks exhausted but happy. I don't know if he has consciously chosen to remain silent about his achievements because we were witness to them, or because those times—the times he was absent from us—don't matter as much as the times we were together.

But they do matter. Those times are a part of my father—his years on council, the success of his business, the charity work, his energy, passion and fearlessness. Knowing now about my grandfather, Tatte, and about my father's life in the camps and all that had been taken from him and all that he has built, his deep-seated need to thank Australia and help the poor and the lonely seem vital to his story. Now, at precisely the point in his life when illness demands that he stop giving and start taking again, *now* seems the perfect time to talk about his selflessness.

Because when I was a teenager—when I was *there* and it was all happening—I didn't want to know. I didn't want to hand out how-to-vote cards on street corners, or go door-knocking and introduce myself to Caulfield residents as the daughter of the man they should vote into council. I didn't want to miss the latest episode of my favourite sitcom because I had to sit through another interminable Council meeting, or spend the night on the phone calling strangers to beg a few dollars for an orphanage in Israel. I didn't want to eat Hungarian goulash with sixty-five-year-olds who pinched my cheeks and pointed out my father's name on the plaques that graced the walls of the Jewish social club he helped found.

I knew my father did all these things and I knew that they were good things. I just didn't see how they related to me.

My father is sitting at his desk. I sit opposite him, staring at the portrait that hangs on the wall behind him: my father in Mayoral robes. On either side of the portrait my mother has hung a number of certificates in recognition of my father's voluntary work for the community and a swag of awards. My father's certification as a Justice of the Peace sits atop the portrait.

'So, are we up to date?' I ask my father, pulling a black, leather-bound scrapbook down from the bookshelf.

We flip through the pages together. Yellowing newspaper clippings, faded photos and discarded speeches complete my father's story, prematurely ended in Fiji. The empty scrapbook I purchased to commemorate his election as mayor of the City of Caulfield in 1988 was, in retrospect, as much a gift for me. By scanning newspapers, sorting photos, cutting and pasting and ordering his life, I was binding myself to my father, to his successes, achievements and dreams.

The scrapbook strains with the weight of memory. We flip to the last entry on the second-last page—a half-page Australia Day article in the local newspaper featuring a photo of my father with a wide smile, holding up his Citizen of the Year Award, Louis and Berti, blurred in the background behind him. The last page remains empty, reserved for the death notice.

An uncomfortable silence settles on the dusty pages.

He's not in the mood to tell any more stories. Maybe the challenges he now takes on every day render less significant everything that came before. My father thumbs the pages back to 1969 and smiles at a faded photo of him and my mother dressed as flamenco dancers, Berti and Mary beside them in matching Chinese dress, Louis and his wife, Ruth, a chef and French maid. A caption in my handwriting, 'The Theodor Herzl Social Club New Year's Eve Ball', in red pen above the photo. The first thing my father gave back to the Jewish community was a Czech–Hungarian Jewish social club, a place for the displaced to form new ties, make friends, belong. Funds raised went to Israel. It was Louis' brainchild and my father had to agree—neither of them had fought for the Jewish state's survival; the least they could do was assist the country financially. By the time my father retired as chairman, the club was the second-largest Jewish social club in Australia.

'The eight hours a week I skipped work to attend meetings never seemed like enough ...'

A sheet of translucent ricepaper adorned with Japanese

calligraphy spills from the scrapbook, a letter of appreciation from the mayor of Ogaki thanking my father for joining the two municipalities as sister cities. I return it to its place beside a photo of my father, beaming as host of his city's seventy-fifth birthday celebration.

'Big smile,' I say. 'Did you really enjoy those council functions, or did you go because you had to?'

'I looked forward to every one of them,' he answers without a trace of sarcasm. 'Every cocktail party and fancy soirée. Not because of the gourmet food or the chance to have my photo taken, but because those functions were peopled by community leaders, business tycoons and politicians, men and women I learnt so much from. I felt alive in that atmosphere, driven to think, propelled to do more and be more. And it wasn't just the big names and important people I learnt from. It was the city planners, the people who managed the parks, the rate collectors and those in charge of waste. They were the people I spent most time with and to thank them—though it wasn't a popular move—when I became mayor, I invited them, all of middle management, to our functions, functions previously closed to all but the top echelon. I'd always been a first-name basis kind of guy. The war had convinced me of one thing: all men are created equal. I wasn't inferior, as the Nazis would have had me believe in the camps, just as fifty years later in Australia, I wasn't any better than the men who cleaned my street.'

My father closes the scrapbook and looks at me.

'My struggles, the fights I fought, and the success I achieved are immaterial. How I built the business, what I achieved for Caulfield, how I treated those I dealt with—that's how you

April 1998

tell what kind of a man I am. And in turn I measure myself by you. I look in your eyes and see how much you love me, and how badly you want me to stick around, and I know that I must've done something right.'

❦

I place the scrapbook back on the bookshelf.

'Do you have any regrets?' I ask.

'Just one,' he answers. 'I wish I'd taken mum and you three kids overseas.'

Photo albums labelled Vietnam, the Panama Canal, Alaska and Mexico line my parents' living-room bookshelf. They'd traded pencils for beads with the tribesmen of the Amazon and trekked Nepal. They'd photographed African children at play and watched elephants laze in the Kenyan sun. Every now and then, they'd taken Peter, Gary and me with them. I knew my father wasn't talking about adventure travel. He was referring to Porubka.

'After my heart bypass operation,' he continues, 'after I sold the jewellery business in 1993, I planned to take you all on a grand European tour, to show you where it all began. I lay in bed at night, dreaming up itineraries: we'd tour Auschwitz, face the plank beds, hospital and crematoria together. Then Porubka: the synagogue, general store, my old school. I wanted to row together from St Gilgen to the Lighthorse Inn, and buy popcorn at the Prague Circus.'

My father pauses, waits for the right words to come.

'Here in Australia, you're so cut off from your history, and our family is so small. I wanted you to know that you were part of something bigger.'

I take my father's hand.

'But we did know,' I say. 'You flew us to Europe to spend summers with our aunts, uncles and cousins.'

'Yes,' my father admits. 'You knew your relatives. You just didn't know me.'

⚘

Our dialogue helps me make sense of the disease my father lives with everyday. I need to make sense of it. I need to find an upside.

The upside is, I now know my father's favourite colour. I know what he dreams about at night and where he first made love. The upside is, his illness taught me the importance of friendship and family and love. The upside is, he made me strong and encouraged me to trust in that strength.

Twenty

DECEMBER 2001

Popping the clear brown capsule from its plastic casing, she pierces its skin with the point of a kitchen knife and squeezes the thick, clear gel into a measuring cup. She adds water and stirs. She turns to her list, though she knows the order by heart. Mogadon next, then vitamin B6. She's been doing this for four years: pouring medicines, herbs and vitamins into her husband. Peeling the indigestible plastic coating off capsules, crushing tablets, measuring morphine, dispensing temazepam — she could do it with her eyes closed. Still, she double-checks.

My mother guides my father to the kitchen table, lowers him into his padded chair. He's getting heavy, less secure on his feet. Twice he has fallen. Powerless, she watched him crash to the floor in slow motion, horrified. She ran up the street, shouting until she found a neighbour at home. Together they got him back on his feet, back in the chair on the soft doughnut pillow. She wiped up the blood, all the while apologising.

For what? That it wasn't her who got the disease?

She tucks a cushion behind his neck, drapes a tea-towel over his trouser legs and unbuttons his shirt. Dad stares straight ahead. If the grandchildren are visiting she'll let them trickle the medicine down his feeding tube, measure the 300 ml of water needed to thin his diet supplement, swirl it round in a cup and tip it into the tube.

It's been a year since they dined together. Now she eats alone, pulled from her plate by his buzzer to adjust a pillow, dim the lights, bring the bottle. She never finishes a meal. She's lost eight kilos. She was skinny to start with.

Feeding tires him, so she puts him to bed, manoeuvring his body by pulling at a leg, wrapping herself around him and tugging gently. Sliding and straining, they ignore the alternative, tucked in the corner of the lounge room—a mechanical arm, pulleys and ropes. It reminds her of a crane.

She flips a switch and suctions his tongue, his teeth, his throat. Saliva bubbles up the plastic tube and is spirited away into a bucket. She pulls the filter from his tracheostomy tube, and takes a pair of yellow, sterilised gloves from their box. She snaps the fingers and grabs a clean catheter, attaches it to the suctioning device, and feeds it down the hole in his throat until it meets resistance. Twirling it between thumb and forefinger, she slowly guides the catheter out, listening and watching until it is clear, sucking only air. Then she stops.

They rise from his bed together and shuffle towards the bedroom wall where she props his body up, lifting his head and steadying him for the trip to the toilet. He goes once a day without much difficulty. The laxatives help because he has no muscles to push. My mother reaches behind him and presses two buttons, activating first a high-powered flushing device to clean him, then a blower to dry him.

They return to the bedroom. Half-sitting, half-standing by the edge of the bed, he lets her undress him, slip his pyjama top on and help him back to bed. She's tired but it doesn't cross her mind to skip a step. She pulls clean strips of gauze from a packet and tucks the rectangles around the feeding tube, brushing the soft freckled skin of his belly with her fingers. Does he still enjoy her touch? She reapplies adhesive so the tube won't rub at his pyjama top and buttons him up. She lays him down gently and slides the night bottle into place.

His skin is still dry from the radiation treatment administered to slow his saliva, and his lips are chapped, so she spoons a dollop of vitamin E cream onto his face. She massages it in, tracing the contour of his lips with her finger, trying to provoke a smile. Sometimes it works. She notices a bed sore erupting on his left ear, reaches for the antiseptic and makes a mental note to mention it to Gary. Glasses off, hearing aid out, towel under the chin, bed control and buzzer within his grasp, blankets smoothed. She recites the checklist in her head.

I poke my head around the door. It's almost midnight. I see my mother reach down, smooth my father's hair and kiss him on the forehead, cheeks, and finally his lips.

'Buzz if you need me,' she whispers, dimming the lights.

'What do you miss?' I ask my mother.

It's midnight and the house is quiet. My father is asleep,

the ventilator breathing for him. His face is slack, shiny, massaged and moisturised. His hands are frozen on rectangles of foam, the bedsheets pulled taut so as not to wrinkle. He has a crush of pillows under his head and a buzzer trapped under his hand. The bed drips with tubes and electrical cord. A bottle pokes from his pyjamas, stained yellow.

I've brought my children to sleep at my childhood home because my husband is away for the weekend and because this impromptu slumber party allows me and my mother time to talk. She is free after midnight.

Josh is asleep on the sofa bed in my brothers' old room, curled up like a question mark. Tanya squirms on the sofa's discarded cushions on the floor, burrowing a hole in which to sink her dreams. Remy sleeps an infant's sleep—eyes fluttering, chunky limbs pitching at the cot's four walls.

'I miss holding his hand,' my mother whispers. 'I miss his touch. I miss him holding me. That feeling of connectedness.'

She closes her eyes and images of 'before' skitter across her eyelids.

I expected her to say she missed the stimulation of work or uninterrupted sleep, a moment in the sun or a meal shared with friends.

She misses nothing, except him.

Her life is timetables and tracksuit pants, her world confined to the four walls of their house. She cannot argue with her husband because she does not want to upset him. Nor can they make love. She has carers come for a few hours each morning so that she can shop at the supermarket, race to the chemist, collect the dry-cleaning.

She cries in private and smiles at her grandchildren, insisting they sleep over, making them scrambled eggs for breakfast before their Papa's day begins. She takes one day at a time, refusing to think of tomorrow, of a life without him. She wipes the sleep from his eyes and the spit from his mouth and prays to God to let her care for her husband like this till they both grow old.

She comes to terms with loss every day, continually adjusting her expectations. She looks for pleasure, curiosity, anger and impatience in her husband's face, trying to read his thoughts and anticipate his needs, to spare his hands the effort of a request. She tells him he's beautiful.

She picks flowers for his desk, to bring the outside in, and develops reams of colour film—Emil in bed, Emil being fed, Emil mid-suction—to keep him permanently with her. She reads medical journals instead of *Time* magazine and smiles when friends remark on her husband's courage and strength.

No one asks how she's doing.

He wrote her a letter. Something she could hold on to after he'd gone. He hoped it would help her reach out to him when she felt most alone. He hoped its message would give her strength. He asked me to take the letter away and have it laminated. He didn't want the type to fade and, with it, the memory of its message.

It was a gift:

My darling Judy

You asked me yesterday what I wish for you. You wanted to know how to live your life. How to construct a future that would honour my memory and keep us close. Our life together and especially these last five years have secured me a place in your heart. I know and I see your devotion daily. Nothing you can do can diminish that.

What I want is for you to be happy; I've caused you too much sadness already. I don't want you to mourn me; you've mourned enough. We have lots of good friends, people who love you. You need to accept their love once I'm gone. You need to say 'yes' when they invite you out ... which they will.

Take control of your life. Don't wait for the pain to go. Work if you want to, travel, study. If our home seems too big or too lonely, sell it. I'll go with you wherever you choose to settle. If you'd rather renovate, strip away any haunting memories with the wallpaper.

See the kids and our grandchildren. Have them over for Friday-night dinners, even if they make a mess. Go to school concerts, sports competitions, grandparents' day and the park. Buy them an ice-cream cone for me.

If you meet a man and he's good to you and kind, allow yourself the possibility of a future. You are young and beautiful and your life mustn't end with me.

It's not easy to recreate yourself. I did it. You can, too.

I love you,
Emil

She didn't need his permission to continue living, to find happiness without him, to laugh again, to love again. But he knew that without those words she would interpret loneliness as loyalty, and confuse celibacy for devotion.

Twenty-one

NOVEMBER 2002

'If you had twenty-four hours of good health given to you, what would you do?' I ask my father. He smiles at the thought.

'I would bend down and kiss my grandchildren.'

A lovely answer, but I want more.

'Okay, I'd wake at 5.00 a.m.,' he types, 'and head to the golf course. After eighteen holes, your mother and I would collect the grandchildren and the rest of the day would be theirs. We'd have a picnic lunch, go to the park, maybe take a tram ride to the beach. There would be piggy-back rides and ice-cream cones and sand-castle competitions. I'd carry the little ones to the car and hoist the older ones onto my shoulders. We'd drive home for dinner and I'd bribe them for kisses with spoonfuls of warm mashed potato and schnitzel. There would be bedtime stories, hugs and kisses and a honey cake and hot chocolate bedtime feast.'

He is enjoying this.

'With Edith at home, Judy and I would be free to go out for dinner. You'd come, of course, with Shaun, Peter, Amanda, Lesley and Gary. I'd have made reservations somewhere quiet, so we could talk and I'd talk until you were sick of the sound of me. I'd tell you how proud I am of you. I'd ask if you were happy with your lives and listen to your answers. I'd try and help make things better if you needed me to. I'd say sorry for not being around as much as I would have liked.'

I read the text out loud, each word as it scuds across the LightWriter's display panel.

'I'd drive Judy home from the restaurant, the long way, across bridges, along the water's edge, past our first home, enjoying Melbourne, saying goodbye. It would be midnight by the time we got home. I'd make strong coffee and Judy would drink hers sitting on my lap. We'd go to bed, but not to sleep. We'd talk until dawn and I wouldn't take my hands off her. I'd hug my wife all night.'

Imagine having twenty-four hours left to live, and only wishing to do what you'd done a hundred times before. Because your dreams were your reality, there *was* nothing better.

For my father, death now makes more sense than life. It hurts to hear him say this, knowing how much he loves life and how hard he's fought to stay alive.

It was an easy decision when the specialists offered him a feeding tube. He chose to forgo the taste, texture and smell of his favourite meals to guard against choking. When his arms grew weak, life still made sense without golf. He found a way to live without his hands, allowing others to dress and toilet him.

'I've still got you guys,' he told us. He survived without his car and later without a voice; life was still wonderful because we were in it together.

Now his fingers are giving up and he traces letters on his trouser leg with his forefinger, hoping we guess at the words before he's forced to spell out the sentence. He's in bed most of the day with the ventilator switched on. He can't get up to pee any more. I try not to remember his wishes, spelt out so clearly that day in his study: 'When I'm bed bound and kept alive by machines, I want to go.'

He reminds us now, tracing 'It's nearly time' on the striped cloth of his pyjama pants. He's trying to prepare us.

I watch him lying on his bed, covered with electrical cords. It's getting harder to hug him, tricky to land a kiss on his cheek amid the tubing. His eyes are closed a lot of the time. He's too tired to type and too weak to sit up and watch the grandchildren play.

I talk. About the kids, Shaun, my father's life. It's hard talking when nothing comes back, but I try. When there's nothing left to say, I stay a while longer, stroking his hair or holding his hand.

I don't like to let go. He feels so far away when we're not touching or talking. He feels it too: the connections being severed. He knows he's close to being entirely cut off. Locked in. He doesn't fear the end, just the silence.

He wants to go before we're totally lost to each other. Death makes more sense.

November 2002

They gave him six months and he's taken five years. He beat all estimates, but battles are tiring.

'You have to give him permission to stop fighting,' I tell my mother. 'He needs to know he's earned the right to die.'

There's silence on the other end of the phone; my mother wishing she could push the truth away and propel me back to childhood. I didn't want to have this conversation over the telephone. I didn't want to have this conversation.

She can't see it's over. She doesn't want to.

'He needs to know you understand. He needs to feel he's done good and that we don't expect any more from him.'

All I can hear is her breathing. I persist.

'I don't want Dad to die feeling ashamed, feeling that he's let us down. Last Friday I asked him how he was feeling. Dad hasn't smiled much lately, and I suddenly felt so far away. Asking was the only way I knew to get him back.'

Silence.

'He told me he's suffering. That when he's not reliving the past he's thinking about the future. About death.'

I hesitate.

'He typed the words "sometimes I want to die".'

My mother asks me how I responded.

'I told him that he's my hero. That I'm proud of him. That he should be proud of himself.'

Twenty-two

FEBRUARY 2003

My father has just traced the word 'soon' on his pant's leg. I look at my mother.

'He wants to die,' she explains. 'In a week.'

Dad has contracted an infection. He turns blue if the ventilator is detached from his tube, even for a moment. He is bed-ridden and hasn't touched his LightWriter in days.

My father resumes his instructions. I can't follow the sweep of his finger, can't make out the first letter, hovering invisible on his pyjama pants, so I offer an alternative.

'First word, first letter ... *A* ... *B* ... *C* ...' I run through the alphabet until he blinks at *M*; a sad game of charades. Two minutes into the game and I guess at the offering: 'Mum is great.'

I agree and promise to look after my mother.

February 2003

My brothers join me at my father's bedside and we camp out in Dad's room all day Monday, Tuesday and Wednesday. We return home only to sleep. We eat meals, telephone for babysitters and cancel commitments from the safety of our parents' double bed, frightened to leave even for a moment. We reminisce about our childhood, transporting Dad back to a time when he could hold us and shape our world.

His carers come, but sit in the next room. Death is too intimate. Dad is wet. Sweat streaks his hair and stains his pillow. He hasn't been to the toilet for two days and my mother asks my brothers to carry him there. They are not even past the bedroom door before they head back. Dad is blue, ice-blue. My brothers lie him down and reconnect the ventilator.

'I'm not ready for you to go,' I tell my father, 'but I know why you need to.'

He needs to take control.

His eyes flicker open.

'I think you are so brave, doing this.' I tell him.

I can't bear the thought that he might feel he's disappointing us. I don't want him to think we see this as giving up.

I wipe his forehead with a damp cloth and ask my mother and brothers to leave the room.

I lie down on my mother's side of the bed and look at my father, so unafraid. I follow the curve of his Roman nose, the bump, just like mine. His hair, usually brushed straight, is now curly with sweat. I realise where my corkscrew curls come from. I see my pale, freckled skin in his. I wonder if I have his courage.

I wake Thursday morning at 5.30 to the phone. It's Gary.

'Come quick,' he says. 'Dad is worse.'

But I can't. I can't move. I know if I get dressed and go, I'll see my father die.

'You have to go,' Shaun forces me out the door, into my car.

My father is blue when I arrive. Gary is cutting away his pyjamas. They can't lift him. Peter produces an absorbent pad and they slip it, with difficulty, under his bottom. Someone mentions the word nappy and I look at my father and know that he's right: it's time.

The sun is up but the room feels dark. Our partners arrive: Shaun, Amanda and Lesley.

'I've taken off work,' Shaun whispers, taking my hand, and I crumble. He's cancelled his patients. It's going to happen today.

Mum rushes past, on the telephone. She's calling friends, the rabbi, doctors.

'He wants it to happen now,' she says.

I feel sick. He was meant to wait a week.

Within half an hour the house is full. My father's oldest and dearest friends sit in the lounge room and line the corridors.

My mother ushers them into my father's bedroom, one at a time, to say their final goodbyes. Dad can't take his friends' hands or turn to look at them, so he blinks at them and in acknowledging them says thank you, and I love you, and goodbye.

Louis hangs back. I walk him into my father's room.

'He can hear you. Talk to him,' I whisper, retreating to the hallway.

'It's been a privilege,' I hear Louis say.

It's hard to find the words, but they do. His friends emerge from the bedroom, some alone, some in pairs, with red eyes and heavy hearts.

'I told him I love him,' Berti tells me. Mary takes her husband's hand and they walk out, grateful to have each other.

❧

The rabbi arrives and the remaining visitors disperse. We go in to my father, glad to have him to ourselves again.

My father is not a religious man. He hasn't sought to ease his departure with thoughts of meeting his maker. Still, he wants to leave this earth having done some good. So, when his rabbi enters the bedroom—not to pray for my father's soul, but to praise it—I can't help but smile.

'You've done good, Emil,' the rabbi tells him. 'You go to God pure. He will look after you.'

How does this man know what God will do? And does it matter?

The rabbi begins to sing a song, soft and mournful, and I think, how nice to leave like this, even if you don't believe.

❧

The rabbi leaves as the doctors arrive. My mother had been putting off calling in the palliative-care team because calling them meant her husband was dying. She had gotten through the past five years because she hadn't allowed herself to think of 'tomorrow'. Now they come, with bags full of death's hidden helpers, and she has to let them in.

'Do you want the ventilator switched off today?' the specialist asks my father.

Dad clicks once for yes. We all know the code. Once for 'yes'. Twice for 'no'.

Mum jumps in. 'Are you sure, Emil?'

He clicks again. Once.

'You won't change your mind?' She's begging now.

Dad traces the word 'F-I-N-A-L' on his pant's leg.

His doctor leaves the bedside, sensing we need more time. We take it in turns.

I go last. I thank my father for teaching me how to live and promise to keep talking to him.

'If you listen real hard Dad and if you keep very quiet, you'll hear me.' I whisper.

Everyone pours back into the room. Mum is carrying the LightWriter. She places it next to Dad and presses play. My father's instructions, recorded weeks earlier, a few words at a time, fill the room.

'I want to be driven past the Town Hall and then the Theodor Herzl Club.'

The machine betrays no emotion as my father describes the route his dead body will take to its final resting place.

Then my mother plays another excerpt—a message for his friends—to be played later. It's an explanation, why he's chosen now to have the ventilator switched off, an excuse to tell them he loves them.

'Don't be sad for me. I've learnt so much these last two years. Loved so much. Been loved in return. I am a lucky man.'

We listen as the machine bleats out words of thanks and then words of advice, death's lessons.

'Don't be afraid of growing old or becoming ill, my friends. Every experience is an experience worth having. Life with all its limitations, obstacles and pain is still a treasure.'

We are all crying now. Mum switches the LightWriter off and goes to kiss her husband. She expects nothing in return. Not a kiss, not a word. He might smile if he has the energy. Still she puts her cheek to his lips, just to feel their warmth on her skin. And he kisses her.

He hasn't kissed her—kissed any of us—in six months. Physically, he couldn't manage it. And now, moments from death, he raises his lips to her cheek and kisses her. I hear the kiss. Peter does too, and now he hovers above his father's lips, holding his breath, hoping. I watch as my father returns his eldest son's kiss, see his lips rise up to contact his son's stubble. We all get kisses.

❦

The doctor comes in and takes my father's hand, gently explaining what will happen once my father gives the order for the ventilator to be switched off. I look across at Dad. His eyes are dry, his breathing even. He knows he will die in a matter of hours, maybe minutes. This is how he wants it.

❦

He's sleepy now. The morphine the doctor has given him is starting to work. Gary promised Dad a peaceful end; he's kept his word.

'You'll be asleep soon, Emil, and then we'll turn down the machine,' the doctor whispers.

I can't help the tears. We're running out of time. More promises to look after mum, stay close to each other and never forget him. Dad's eyes close to the rush of morphine.

'I love you, Dad,' I shout. And then a chorus of 'I love yous' erupts behind me. We repeat the words over and over, trying to coax him back. My father drifts away to a lullaby of love.

'Say hi to Willie,' I whisper as the ventilator clicks off.

❦

The doctor looks at my mother and nods, as if in answer to a question.

Dead? He can't be.

I look across at my mother and brothers. They're still waiting for the end. For the last gasp. The struggle. A sign.

'He's dead,' the doctor says.

And then I feel it. A slipping away. I look at my father, his body so still, so empty.

He is free.

❦

The tears slow. Dad floats. Mum is still talking to him, trying to tempt him back. She touches her cheek to his lips and waits.

She wants me to touch him, too.

'See? He's still warm.'

But he's not. I hold his hand—for her—but when I look for him, it's in the space above me.

'Bye, Dad,' I whisper at the ceiling.

The grandchildren arrive from school in the afternoon. My father had asked that the children come over, regardless of his situation. It's a Thursday. The grandchildren always come for dinner on Thursday.

'Maybe they want to come in and say goodbye,' my mother offers, but I resist. My children haven't seen death before. I close the bedroom door and head for the hallway to schoolbags and homework and half-eaten lunches.

One hour later, my mother calls me to my father's bedside. I don't want to go in. I want to remember him breathing. She insists and I open the door to see my father's bed, surrounded by children, his sheets littered with drawings. My son Joshua adds his love letter to the pile. He takes his grandfather's hand, kisses it, says goodbye, and leaves the room.

'See, Mum?' my daughter Tanya says, turning to me from the bedside. 'Dead people don't fly away. Papa is still here.'

They've taken the wheelchair out to the backyard to test its grunt. The older grandchildren hang off the back, the smaller ones pressed into the soft bucket seat, shouting 'faster, faster' to the lucky cousin who has the controls. They race around the garden—forward, back, left, right, cutting divots in the grass, whooping with laughter. I can hear them from inside my parents' house and the laughter feels good. I think Dad would like it.

I sleep at my parents' house that night, in my old room. My mother lies in her bed, next to her husband. She needs one last night with him, then she'll call the undertakers. I doubt she'll sleep.

My brothers join us on Friday at dawn. The air is thick with despair. The undertakers follow, eager to commence their work. We excuse ourselves as the men pull on rubber gloves. An hour later they wheel a green body-bag past the open door of my father's study, where I sit with my mother. I hear her cry out.

'He's not in there,' I tell her.

❀

The flag is at half-mast at the Caulfield Town Hall and a dozen councillors line the footpath, waving, as my father's hearse rolls along Glen Eira Road. A bigger crowd spills onto the footpath outside the Theodor Herzl Club. They stand, holding half-eaten bagels, carrying their bridge hands with them. We follow the black station-wagon in my father's car. My mother turns from the front seat to look at me and I take her hand. She can feel it too: Dad is here, leading the convoy, watching and loving it. He has drawn quite a crowd.

We sit on wooden seats at the front of the funeral chapel. The room is too small. It's raining, and hundreds of my father's friends stand, soaked and silent, outside the double doors. The rabbi struggles to his feet.

'He taught us how to live,' the rabbi says, repeating the

final words of my eulogy.

'He taught me, too,' the rabbi adds, before falling silent. He is genuinely upset. This job, this funeral, is personal.

We wait and then the rabbi says something so right and so true it makes me smile.

He says, 'I don't know why there's so much suffering in the world, so much hatred and pain. I don't understand life and I don't understand death. I *do* know that if anyone has the courage to stand before God and say "Enough, already", to stand up and present the case for humanity, it's Emil.'

I imagine my father up there, doing his thing, and I start to heal.

We follow the coffin to the graveside, holding my mother upright between us as the box disappears into the ground. The first clod of earth hits the wood with a thud and my mother buckles.

'He's not in there,' I whisper.

He's here at the funeral, checking out the crowd and checking on Mum, but he's not in that box. Finally freed of disease he has escaped the leaden body that has held him prisoner this past year and the next life is beckoning. I imagine him hovering, stretching his legs that had been so stiff, unfurling his fingers, fanning out his arms.

I don't cry until the end of the service, until a friend reaches out to hug me and I see that she's crying, and then I can't stop. Because I want my father back. And because surrounding me is proof of a successful life. At the end, Dad had said, it all came down to who you loved and who loved you back.

'They love us, Dad,' I whisper into the crowd.

❦

'I won't say goodbye,' my mother tells me. Because, for her, although my father's heart is stopped and his body covered over with earth, he has not died. Not completely.

My father's newfound freedom doesn't make my mother any happier. She misses him, misses his face, expressionless as it was in those final months; and the warmth of his body, motionless in their bed. Two months have passed, but he is still a part of her life: not alive, but present, his slippers still beneath their bed, his toothbrush next to hers in a cup by the basin.

I tell her that moving on is not the same as forgetting, that moving forward without him won't lessen the love that they shared. But she holds tight to the strings tethering him to her world, and refuses to set him free. She knows he can't answer but she talks to him daily, after dark, when they're alone in bed.

The body she tended these last five years is in a grey, granite tomb, but the man she married still keeps her company.

❦

I think about my own family and smile: Remy and the way she delights in water and mud and mess; Tanya in a tutu splashing paint and dreaming in pink; and Josh, his nose in a book, his toothy grin. And Shaun, strong and supportive, pushing me to dream.

'How can I feel this way?' I ask Shaun. 'It's only been two months since Dad's death. Am I heartless?'

Shaun reminds me of the first seven days when I couldn't smile. He reminds me of the darkness I couldn't shift, of the days I spent at my parents' house in funeral attire, sitting on a low stool, receiving visitors. It felt wrong to go out in daylight then. I felt safe cloaked in family and friends and reminiscence.

He reminds me that I am my father's daughter. I think about my father and try to remember a time when he wasn't moving forward.

The war, Willie's death, starting over in Australia, his disease—none of it stopped him. I thought of his strength when ill, how he'd chosen to watch when he could no longer walk, listen when he could no longer talk, and smile through it all, because he still had us. Even at the end he didn't opt out, he took control.

I like the comparison.

Acknowledgements

Grateful thanks to my friends in the Professional Writing and Editing course at RMIT for their intelligence, support and invaluable comments.

To Henry Rosenbloom, thank you for allowing me to tell my father's story.

And with gratitude to my editor, Foong Ling Kong, for her careful reading, valuable insights and expert advice.

And finally, to my husband, Shaun, and our three children, Josh, Tanya and Remy, for their encouragement, enthusiasm and infinite patience.